THE INSPIRED WOMAN

How to Use Your Faith and Receive Everything You Want in Life

Cyndi L. Greene

10-10-10 Publishing

THE INSPIRED WOMAN
How to Use Your Faith and Receive Everything You Want in Life
www.theinspiredwomanbook.com

Paperback ISBN: 979-8-333634-10-8

Publisher
10-10-10 Publishing
Markham, ON Canada

Printed in Canada and the United States of America

I dedicate this book to my parents, Cecil and Janette Lampkin, who are no longer with us, but their love and belief in me will always shine bright. They taught me to always give my best and never quit! I am the woman I am today because of them!

Contents

Acknowledgements

I would first like to give thanks to my **LORD and SAVIOR, YESHUA,** for giving me the revelation from HIS Word to write this book. When HE first spoke to me, and said, "Now is time to write the book!" I was so confused as to what to do next, but HE didn't leave me there; HE slowly opened my understanding and walked me to the path needed to find the publishing company that would help me fulfill and complete the mission.

I would like to thank my dear husband, **Jeffrey L. Greene**, who has been by my side for over 35 years and believed in me through all my entrepreneur endeavors—some good, some bad—but he never gave up on me. I love you always.

I am grateful for my daughters, **Stephanie and Joi**. You are so special to me. Seeing both of you becoming beautiful women and walking in your call and purpose, makes me so proud and happy to have you in my life.

Thank you to all my **friends and family**, who always believed in me and supported me with their love and wisdom. All those late-night talks, tears, and laughter we shared; I will always remember.

I would like to thank **Gloria Mayfield Banks**. That 30-minute cassette tape you made, "90 Days to Get Your Grand Am," forever changed my life. I learned for the first time that I could achieve my goals if I just take it one step at a time! You taught me that consistency will always pay off! I can't thank you enough.

Apostle Dr. Kim Neuhaus, I am so grateful that GOD used you to help me see and accept the call HE placed on me. You showed me the mantle of my grandfather, Bishop George W. Martin, and why it was important for me to step into it. Thank you.

Dr. John Maxwell, your leadership books helped me to understand true leadership. I didn't know I was a leader until you taught me that leadership is serving. Now when I do anything, I always ask myself first, "How can I serve?" Thank you.

Cheryl Jackson, I love your praise and worship every time I listen to you on the radio. I can go all the way in and give GOD the praise until I sweat my hair out! You touch so many lives and help us to love one another as we love CHRIST!

LaTasha Briscoe, thank you for creating the Sweatpants and Chill event! You allowed me to be myself, showing me that it's okay to conduct business in sweats! I met so many powerful women who shared their hearts and poured into me the confidence to embrace my uniqueness.

Shanda Sumpter, I wish I had your energy! Thank you for loving both YESHUA and business together. It was so refreshing to know I do not have to compromise my faith to do business.

Lola Tomorrow, I thank you for always keeping it real! You keep me rooted and grounded in knowing that I can be successful in my business no matter what I might be going through.

Foreword

In May of 2023, I had the pleasure of meeting Cyndi Greene when she registered for my booking writing challenge. I knew right then and there that she was going to be one of my most successful students. Her smile and bubbly personality touched my heart so much that I gladly agreed to write this foreword for her.

She has a work ethic that I haven't seen in a while, to stay the course no matter what obstacles come her way. I witnessed her commitment and devotion to getting this book out to you, because she cares so much about seeing you grow and receive everything you want in life.

There is no doubt in my mind that you will have an amazing transformation in your life as a result of reading *The Inspired Woman*.

Your faith will elevate so high, you will think that you just left planet Earth! Your mind will expand to new heights and depths, that will break strongholds that were holding you back from receiving all the beautiful things and experiences life has to offer.

I am confident that the inspiring stories Cyndi shares with you will strengthen your faith-walk, and magnify the love you have in your heart.

Raymond Aaron
***New York Times* Bestselling Author**

Chapter 1

This Is Not Your Typical Book on Faith

"For the LORD giveth wisdom; out of HIS mouth cometh knowledge and understanding."
(Proverbs 2:6 KJV)

Who Told You Faith Was Easy?

Have you ever wondered why you don't think the same as everybody else? Do you always feel things, and those around you don't understand why you feel a certain way? No matter what you do, you just don't fit in.

We will take you on a journey that will take you deep into the recessions of your inner being, the true self, the real you, called your spirit.

In this true place of your inner spirit, lies everything that is real, true, and eternal. It is a place not talked about much, nor are you encouraged to go there. Its origins began in the book of Genesis, from the very thought of GOD. It's a very narrow path of discovery and many do not find it.

It's called FAITH!

Yes, we all have heard of it, but do we really know the depths of it? What is faith? The Merriam-Webster Dictionary defines faith as: 1) allegiance to duty or a person; loyalty, 2) belief and trust in GOD, 3) complete trust, 4) a system of religious beliefs.

All these definitions explain the world's view on what faith is, but is it GOD'S intended spiritual understanding of what faith is?

We are going to go deeper, much deeper than this. We were told to "just have faith" or "just keep the faith," but no one gave us a step-by-step blueprint on how to just keep the faith. The Bible says, "If you have faith the size of a mustard seed, you can speak to the mountain and tell it to be removed into the sea and it shall obey you. If this is so easy to do, why haven't we done it? Why are the mountains in our lives still here? Who told us it would be easy? Where did this lie come from?

Faith is small like a mustard seed, and it's eternal; it's from the beginning like Genesis.

You cannot stay in surface level understanding and operate in true faith. You must go deep; you must go inward, into spiritual understanding, to operate in this real mustard seed faith.

I Tried It Once and It Didn't Work

In January 1999, my husband and I attended a revival. The man of God said, "It's your time to go and get your house." We were living in an apartment at the time. We went to the apartment complex office and told the manager that we would be moving out in 30 days. Then we started looking at homes. Every day, we went out to different areas to look at homes. We knew we were going to find our home.

We put in several applications, but nothing came through. Days and days went by, but still no contract. It was now 30 days later, and we had to tell the rental office that we were not moving. The rental office manager said to us, "You must move because we've already rented out your apartment; you must be out of the apartment by tomorrow." I was in shock! I couldn't believe it. Now we had a major problem on our hands. We only had 24 hours to pack up everything and find a place to stay.

I was so overwhelmed; I didn't know what to do. I couldn't focus on buying a home because I now had to focus on finding a place to stay in 24 hours. Looking back on it now, I realized I didn't understand faith. I didn't know how to use my faith correctly. I did it all wrong. I didn't even understand why my faith didn't work.

Have you ever wanted something so bad that you just jumped in headfirst? That's what we did. We were so excited about becoming a homeowner that we forgot to invite GOD into our plans, or better yet, ask GOD what HIS plan for us was.

I thought I knew what faith was. I thought all I had to do was believe and then do the work—just go out and do the work and it would happen. What I didn't understand was that GOD has always had a plan for our lives, and HIS plan is far above our thoughts and understanding.

Sometimes, we get so focused on what we want, we don't realize that GOD has a plan that is superior to anything that we could ever imagine. We think we know GOD'S plan and it's going to be just the way we want it to be, but that's not how GOD operates.

I thought that I could just say I want something, believe I'm going to get it, and bam, it's done. That's not how GOD operates. The Word of GOD says, *"Trust in the LORD with all thy heart, and lean not to thy own understanding, but in all thy ways acknowledge Him, and He will direct thy path" (Proverb 3:5 KJV).*

I made several mistakes. Wanting a home was my earthly desire. I never asked GOD if it was HIS will at this time for me to own a home. I just went into my thoughts of what I wanted, went to the rental office, and told them we would be moving out in 30 days. Never once did I stop and ask the LORD if this was HIS will for us at this time or if we should wait. When I read the scripture in Jeremiah 29:11, it said, *"For I know the thoughts that I think toward you, saith the LORD, thoughts of peace, and not of evil, to give you an expected end."* I learned that faith does not work when it isn't real faith. Real faith seeks the will of the LORD and always line up with the Word of GOD.

I Watched My Mama Do It

There is no love like a mama's love. Your mama loves you so much that she will do anything to protect you. I come from a large family. I have seven siblings. We grew up in a small country town in Michigan. My mother came from a large family also. She had 11 brothers and sisters, most of whom lived in the Detroit area. Her parents were married for over 50 years, and her father, Bishop George W. Martin, pastored a church in the metropolitan Detroit area. My mother was raised in the Apostolic Church.

When she married my father, they moved to a small town in the country. At that time, I thought growing up in the country was very hard. But now I see that we were raised with strong work ethics and strong values. I don't see that as much today.

My mother had some fears about driving. I felt those fears, but I didn't know why I had those same fears when I started driving. It wasn't until I heard her story that I finally received clarity and understanding of what happened to her and how it was transferred to me.

When I was around seven years old, my mother hit a pedestrian, who later passed away.

When my mother would drive, and the road conditions were icy, slippery, or there was a lot of snow on the road, or any kind of challenge with driving, my mother would start praying and calling on the name of YESHUA.

As kids, my siblings and I used to, in our playtime, imitate her. We would act like we were her, and we would call on the name YESHUA and then bust out laughing. We would do this every time we saw our mother do this. As I got older and on my own, I realized what my mother was doing—she knew that there was power in the name of YESHUA. When she did not have time to pray long prayers but needed the power of GOD to operate in her situation right then, she knew to call on the name of YESHUA, and so she did. Because my mother did this, I learned this and used it in my adult life.

When I moved to Maryland after experiencing major abuse and trauma in a relationship that left me homeless and pregnant, I started using drugs after my baby was born.

My drug use spiraled out of control as I got high 24/7, 365 days a year. I went from marijuana, to alcohol, to cocaine. I did whatever I could get my hands on. One day I was driving back from a trip with my 3-year-old daughter in the back seat, in Washington, DC. This was during the time when car seats were optional for kids. My daughter was bouncing and playing in the back seat like she was never going to be still again, when suddenly, she lay down and fell asleep. When I looked in my rear mirror and saw her asleep, I heard satan whisper in my ear, "Now you can go get your drugs before you get home." So that's what I did. I drove up to a dealer on the street, rolled down my window, and purchased a small bag of marijuana. I put it in my pocket and drove off. As I was waiting for the light to turn green, I looked in my rearview mirror and noticed two police cars that were two cars behind me. I felt in my gut that they were coming for me. Now, I must tell you I didn't know GOD at this time, so I called it my "gut," when in fact it was my spirit that was warning me. As the light finally turned green and I started to move forward, indeed the police turned on their sirens, moved close on my bumper and motioned for me to pull over. When I did, the officer came up to my window and asked for my driver's license and registration. When I handed it to him, he asked me, "What are you doing over here?" I was so nervous, I tried to come up with a lie that I thought would help my current situation, so I said I was lost and was trying to find my sister's house.

He took my information and went back to his cruiser. I looked again in my rearview mirror, and I saw him arguing with the other officer about the fact that I had a baby in my car, and what they were going to do with the baby.

At that point, I realized how serious this was, and that I might be going to jail. So, I asked myself, "Who can get me out of jail?" But I realized that wasn't the right question to ask. The right question to ask was, "Who can keep me from going to jail?" That's when I remembered my mother and how she would call on YESHUA when she needed HIM right then. The answer to my last question had only one correct answer, and HIS name is YESHUA! I started crying and calling on HIS name to help me; I kept on calling with a sincere heart, with all my heart, like I had never called anybody's name before.

When that officer came back to my window, I wiped my face and looked at him, expecting to have to beg for forgiveness, but he said, "This is what will happen. You will give me what you have, and we will let you go. If you don't give it to me, we will search your car, we will find it, and your baby will become a ward of the state. Your car will be impounded, and you will go to jail!" I froze. I couldn't believe what I was hearing. I knew he would find it, because it was in my right pocket. My mind was racing, with my thoughts flying everywhere. "What should I do? My brother went to jail for a year just for having a small bag. I'm in DC and have heard many bad stories about cops in

DC—do I trust them?" I didn't know what to do, but once again, my gut, or really my spirit, said, "Give it to him." So, I did. He poured it out on the street and said, "Now you get out of here and don't come back."

I drove away and it seemed like I didn't blink the whole way home! My daughter slept through the whole ordeal; she never woke up to see her mom in this situation. When I got home and sat on my bed, I couldn't believe I was free and that I wasn't going to jail!

I saw the power of faith that had operated in my mother, that I used to play with, save me from a life-changing moment that could have destroyed my future and my daughter's future.

GOD IS REAL! HIS WORD is real; it will do that which it is sent out to do. Even when you don't know HIM yet as LORD and SAVIOR, it still cannot return void; it must do what it says it will do.

My mom is no longer here with me, but this was one lesson I will never forget, and I will pass it on to my children and theirs. Whenever you have an emergency and need the power of GOD to show up in that very moment, always call on HIS name.

The Bible says, *"Train a child in the way they should go, and when they are old, they shall not depart from it."* I saw that scripture operate in my life. That scripture saved my life. My mother released her faith; she believed and knew that GOD would save her in a moment of a twinkle, and HE did every time.

She taught us that no matter how bad it looks, when you call on JESUS, everything will change. My mama had the faith and belief to move mountains. If you were touched by this story, I have some free resources for you on my website. Go to www.theinspiredwomanbook.com to get a support guide for women who struggle with addiction of any kind.

She Got It and I Didn't

Do you ever wonder why good things happen for some people and bad things happen for others? Have you ever experienced wanting something so bad that you say, "I'm going to work hard to attain this," only to see someone else have it just handed to them. You start to ask yourself, "Why did she get it and I didn't?" Then you go into even more self-doubt and sadness, because you don't understand what happened.

There could be many reasons why you did not receive the thing you wanted the most, but the truth is, everything we have has a time and a season, which is not on our time but on GOD'S time. The Bible says that GOD wants to give us good gifts, but HE cannot give you more than you can handle. HE does not want it to be a stumbling block to you. He prepares us so that when we are ready, the gifts can flow, operate, and will be received with thanksgiving. We can use this time to focus our faith on preparing ourselves to grow stronger in the Word, HIS will, and HIS ways. While you are preparing, you will start to notice that you're getting closer and closer to HIM. The anointing will grow stronger and stronger when you pray and when you worship HIM. Then things will come easier, like peace and joy all around you, more and more. You will stop worrying and wanting. You will learn how to allow the SPIRIT to operate in your thoughts and your actions.

When I was twelve, I went to church two to three times a week. In those days, the pastor instructed us to tarry to be filled with the HOLY SPIRIT. He said "You must repent, confess all your sins, pray, and ask for forgiveness of every wrong thing you have ever done. Then after you have asked for forgiveness, ask to be filled with the HOLY SPIRIT."

One day my neighbor and I were on our knees tarrying for the HOLY SPIRIT. I wanted to be born again so bad; I wouldn't stop until I received it. I remember being on my knees and confessing all my twelve-year-old sins (I hit my brother; I took a piece of gum from my sister... all the things that I knew were wrong that I had done), and I asked the LORD to fill me with HIS HOLY SPIRIT. I wanted to be saved.

The pastor said, "Just say hallelujah, hallelujah, hallelujah, over and over again, and you will be filled with the HOLY SPIRIT, which will be evident by speaking in a new tongue." So, we did that.

After many minutes of tarrying, the pastor came over to us and told my neighbor that she had received the HOLY SPIRIT, and that she was saved. He looked at me and said, "You did not receive it." I put my head down to cry; I felt sadness wash over me, and I asked GOD as I cried, "Why didn't I get it?" Then I heard this voice in my ear. It was not GOD'S voice but satan's, and what he said to me was a pivotal turning point in my life. I was young and I didn't understand spiritual things. I didn't even understand the voice that was speaking to me—I just knew I was unhappy, and I wasn't going to receive what I wanted the most.

You may be asking, "So, what did the voice say to you?" Well, I didn't know it at that time that sometimes that still voice is not your voice or your thoughts, but the enemy trying to kill, steal, and destroy you. I knew I was different than most kids, even my siblings, but I didn't know that my destiny was ordained before I was even born, and for that reason, the evil one's plan from the beginning was to keep me from living the life GOD had destined me to live.

That voice not only said these words to me when I was twelve, but he also said the exact words to me the night I finally did get saved, twenty years later! That evil voice said,

"Don't you see, even GOD doesn't want you; nobody wants you." That voice changed my life for the next twenty years. It caused me to leave the church and I didn't come back until twenty years later.

Little did I know that this was just the beginning of the horrible things the enemy tried to do to keep me from knowing truth and walking in the power of GOD'S love and faith.

I know you have your own stories of how you wanted something so bad that when it didn't happen for you, you felt the world was falling on you. I want you to know that everything has a reason for the season. Even when it seems unbearable to carry on, somehow you find the strength to keep going. That strength comes out of nowhere. It keeps coming and coming.

I'm sure you can look back at something right now that you went through and didn't believe you had the strength to survive it, but you did. That was the HOLY SPIRIT destiny moving you through life to keep you on track for the plans GOD ordained for your life.

How Much Do You Believe?

There will come a time when your faith will be questioned, and you will be at the threshold of deciding to believe or not believe. If you make the wrong decision, deciding not to believe, it could change everything in your life. If you make the decision to believe, it could change everything in your life. When you find yourself at this threshold and you must decide to walk in faith or to run in fear, the only thing you can rely on is your belief and trust in the Almighty GOD.

Sometimes we can use other people's faith and belief to get us through, but there will always be a time when you cannot depend or rely on someone else's strong faith and belief. You are going to be tested. You are going to have to stand on your own belief. When that day comes, you will know it because it will be a life-changing experience.

You may wonder, "How much faith do I need; how much belief do I have to have; do I have enough; how do I know if I have enough?" You will know, because the moment you release it, you will feel something powerful in your spirit that you have never felt before.

The moment before you release it, and that power that you feel when you release your faith, will be when you will start the releasing of the HOLY SPIRIT operating on your behalf in that situation.

We know that GOD is always with us and always guiding us, but HE has given us free will; HE has given us the ability to choose. HE does not force himself on us in any situation.

We must choose to trust HIM or not. Once we make that choice, everything starts the spiritual process of moving on your behalf.

So, how much do you believe? You must ask yourself, "Do I believe GOD no matter what I see with my natural eyes or hear with my natural ears? Do I believe when everything says differently?" Once you decide with all your being and are committed to that decision, your faith will now be operating at a dimensional level that natural man knows nothing about.

This is the same faith that GOD spoke of in Genesis when HE said, "Let there be light." You have just stepped into the realm of faith that GOD used to create the heavens and the earth. By knowing this, you are now "FAITH MANIFESTED!" When you believe faith, you become faith. The Bible says, "Faith is the substance of things hoped for; the evidence of things not seen." Your faith is the substance and the evidence of things not seen. The more you believe, the more the substance of faith operates in you.

The LORD has always given me inspiration and direction through my dreams at night. One night I had a dream; it was a very vivid dream. I was working at a Catholic high school as an accounts receivable clerk. My good friend Linda also worked with me as the accounts payable clerk. We went to lunch together and I told her that I'd had a dream the night before, where I got laid off from my job there at the high school, but then some days later, they called me back to work. The next day, when I saw Linda at work, I told her all about my dream and she was astonished by the information I relayed to her.

It was now Friday of the same week that I'd had the dream, and it was payday. My supervisor called me into her office to inform me that today would be my last day and that I was being let go due to budget cuts; my position was being phased out. She handed me my last paycheck and I packed my things, left the building, and headed home.

When I got home, I called my husband and told him the news, and I started praying that GOD would show me what to do next. I had such peace in my heart that everything was going to be okay.

There was a visiting prophet coming to a church in Baltimore that night, so we decided to go to the service. I praised GOD like I always love to do. We had a wonderful time in the Word that night. Then the prophet said, "Give the best offering you've ever given." I took just a moment and asked GOD, "What shall I give?" I felt the leading of the HOLY SPIRIT to give my whole last paycheck. When I was writing out the envelope and the check, I saw my husband looking at me; his eyes got bigger and bigger when he saw the amount that I was putting on the check to put into the offering, and I knew he was quietly asking me, "What are you doing? Are you putting your whole check in the offering?" I nodded, "Yes!"

I was so nervous, but I knew I had heard the LORD, and I believed without any doubt that this was the right thing to do! So, I did it!

Guess what? On Tuesday, the next week, I got a phone call. It was from my previous employer at the high school. It was my supervisor, and she informed me that the assistant treasurer had quit, and she wanted me to come back to work, but not as a clerk but as the assistant treasurer, with a 20K raise! All praise to YESHUA the CHRIST!

This is how faith operates when we allow the power of faith to move in our lives, even when we don't see anything in the natural world revealing it to us. When I coach my clients on developing their faith to move mountains, I love to show them how total surrender will take them into a realm of trust and belief that this world cannot explain or show them.

Now I Get It!

Everyone has a measure of faith. Some of us know how to use our faith in one area or use our faith in all areas of our lives. You can measure how much faith you have by the words you use every day, the thoughts you have every day, and your actions resulting from those thoughts and words.

I meet people every day and I listen to the words they speak. It is amazing to me when I see so many people curse themselves, just because they speak negative words instead of positive words. The Bible teaches us that *"death and life are in the power of our tongue, and they that use it, will have the fruit thereof."* It also says, *"I have come that you may have life and have life abundant."*

If you are speaking death, how can your words create life? You must decide what you want—health or sickness, and wealth or poverty. Your words must line up with what you want. When the two don't match, it creates nothing, or the opposite of what you want.

I love to see my students speak faith-filled words and come back and tell me that what they were believing GOD for has happened in their life. This brings me such joy because I know it is real and it is true.

You can have this in your life; it's there for the asking. I help women just like you, to go deeper in exploring the innermost desires of your heart and bring it into self-discovery so that you can build a solid foundation of faith and receive everything GOD has planned for your life.

In my 7-step FAITH NOW program, I will walk you through a faith-filled system that will renew your mind with CHRIST-minded revelation and creation to bring you positive results in every area of your life. Go to www.theinspiredwomanbook.com to learn more about this and other programs.

Chapter 2

I Just Realized Who I'm Not

"Let us hold fast the confession of our hope without wavering, for HE who promised is faithful."
(Hebrews 10:23)

I'm in This World, But I'm Not of This World

GOD did not make the world; HE made the earth! In the book of Genesis 1:1, it reads: *"In the beginning, GOD created the heaven and the earth"* (KJV). So, who made the world? The world is the fallen state of the earth after man chose sin over GOD'S original plan for mankind.

HE created us in HIS image and likeness; HE gave us a will and a choice to choose life or death. We know the story in Genesis, how lucifer beguiled Eve and she ate of the tree of good and evil and then shared the fruit with her husband. This action was the beginning of our separation from our creator. This action gave the authority that mankind had on the earth to lucifer, and the world is now led by lucifer and the fallen angels that went with him.

Many people don't believe in the GOD of the Bible, but I do. You must know HIM for yourself, because that is how your faith will grow and become stronger. What do you do to know HIM for yourself? **You must be born again, of the Water and the SPIRIT!**

I still remember the morning after I gave my life to CHRIST. I woke up with a huge smile on my face. My shoulders seemed as light as feathers. I felt FREE for the first time in my life! When I went outside, the sky looked bluer than I had ever seen it look before. I could hear the birds chirping louder than before. I was looking at the trees and the flowers like I had never seen them before. I knew that I was born again! No one and nothing could tell me that GOD wasn't real!

I was experiencing a rebirth, not only in my natural understanding of the physical world I live in, but I was also experiencing a spiritual realm called "the Kingdom of GOD." In the Kingdom, everything operates differently than in the world. It's like you are here in this world, but you're not here in this world. It doesn't make sense; it won't make sense using your physical understanding. It only makes sense when you have chosen to give your life to CHRIST, receive HIS gift of salvation, and be born again of Water and the SPIRIT.

Have you given your life to CHRIST? Do you believe HE is the Son of GOD? If so, then you understand what I just shared with you. If not, it's not too late. I invite you to give your life to CHRIST and become born again into the Kingdom of GOD. It's a gift from GOD, to all that want to be saved! In Acts 2:38, the Bible says, "... 'Repent, and be baptized, every one of you, in the name of YESHUA the CHRIST for the remission of sins, and ye shall receive the gift of the HOLY SPIRIT'" (KJV). HE is waiting on you; HE loves you so much! Your next step is to find a Bible-believing church of the Apostle Doctrine in your area, and they will lead you toward the path to salvation. If you want more information about this, I am always available to share more and support you in your spiritual walk with CHRIST. Reach out to me at: www.theinspiredwomanbook.com.

Not By My Works

Are you a workaholic? I think I was too! Growing up in a large family, we had to start working in the home at age five. Our first job was to wash and dry dishes and put them away. I remember my sister and I standing on chairs washing dishes; there was water on the floor everywhere, and we were trying to reach the cabinets to put the dishes away. We broke a lot of dishes and glasses! Our second job was to learn how to make cornbread. My father loved cornbread. We cooked cornbread every day. The hardest work we had to do was plant and grow a garden. My father didn't use pesticides on the plants; he used our little fingers! We had to remove the bugs with our own hands from the plants every day. This took forever—at least that's how it feels to an eight-year-old. When it was time to harvest all the food, we had to get up early and go out to pick everything: corn, green beans, okra, blackeye peas, onions, tomatoes, eggplant, carrots, collards, and more!

Working in this garden started my entrepreneur career. I didn't understand it when I was a child, but it takes a lot to feed a family of ten, so to off-set that, my father had us get up early on Saturday mornings, pick truckloads of corn and other vegetables, take them into the city, and sell them in the neighborhoods. My job was to knock on the doors and ask them if they would like to purchase fresh vegetables from us, and come out to the truck and select what they wanted. My older siblings would bag everything and collect the money. We would sell out every weekend, and if we didn't, we would give the rest away to help those in need.

When we got home, we would divide all the money into eight piles, and each of us would get one. I was so excited to see how working hard pays off! But all this work didn't define who I really was. I went to college to study business and got my first corporate job as a manager trainee; I worked 70 hours a week, but that still wasn't who I was. Years later, I started my own business and worked even more hours a week; I grew the business to six-figures, and still, that wasn't who I was.

You may think you know who you are, because someone gave you a title, or a position, or even an inheritance, passed down from many generations, but that still doesn't state who the real you is. Once we disclose who we are not, then we can focus on the truth of who we are.

I Am Not Moved by What I See

"While we look not at the things which are seen,
but at the things which are not seen:
for the things which are seen are temporal;
but the things which are not seen are eternal"
(2 Corinthians 4:18 KJV).

Do you make decisions based on information that you receive through your eyes and ears? Sometimes, looks can be deceiving. Your reality is formed from your past experiences and future expectations. We visualize what we remember from our past and what we want in the future. These sights are not always true. Sometimes we move with false information that our eyes showed us, but it wasn't real. There will be times when you will have to stand still and not move at all, so that you can take a second look and see the truth before you move.

Faith is seeing when you don't see. It's like walking in the woods at night with no lights, and it's so dark that you can't even see your hand in front of you. I remember when

I was around ten; at night, my siblings and I would dare each other to ride our bikes and race through the corn stalks to see who would chicken out first. It was so scary, but we did it anyway. I didn't know that this was "playing by blind faith!" It's amazing how things from your childhood represent courage and strength in your adulthood.

Have you ever done something that you couldn't see with your natural eyes, but you did it blind, and everything worked out great? That was blind faith! There is a realm of faith that is not seen with your natural eyes but only with your spiritual eyes. Faith is eternal; it's given to us from our eternal GOD. That is why, when we do things without seeing with our natural eyes but instead allow faith to be our eyes, we move from the natural to the supernatural and allow the eternal SPIRIT of GOD to bring forth everything we now see in the natural.

I Am Not the Tail, I Am Not Beneath

"And the LORD shall make thee the head, and not the tail; and thou shalt be above only, and thou shalt not be beneath; if that thou hearken unto the commandments of the LORD thy GOD, which I command thee this day, to observe and to do them."
(Deuteronomy 28:13 KJV).

Do you see yourself as GOD sees you? You are not the tail; you are not beneath—you are the head and are above only. Don't let the cares of this world determine where you are. Trust and believe only what GOD says about you. If HE says you are not the tail, then it is true. HE is the only one who has made you above and not beneath.

You have everything inside you to rise above anything and everything that comes your way. Never let your circumstances dictate how high or far you can go. You can do so much more than you think you can. It's the power of faith.

Your faith will take you higher and higher in everything that you do. Just believing that you can do a specific thing, immediately raises your belief to higher heights of faith power. Knowing that you are above only, takes you into a spiritual realm that others don't even know exists. This is where you want to be. This is where you want to stay. The more you stay with the mindset of "I am above only," the more your faith will rise and catapult you into unwavering faith; then you will see amazing results happening in every area of your life.

Never say, "I'm down on my luck," or any negative thing that goes against what you really want. The word "luck" is a nickname for lucifer. You are causing a curse to come upon yourself. Anything down or beneath is opposite of GOD'S eternal plan for your life. You must always understand that no matter what it looks like, you are the head, you are above, you are blessed, and you are highly favored! Say these words to yourself every day. Never stop believing them. You are above only!

One day I was working with one of my clients and she told me she was having a bad day. I said, "No, no, you are not having a bad day; you are having a great day!" She looked at me like I was saying something foreign to her. She stared at me with a confused look as if she was saying, "I'm going through so much, and I feel awful, and you're telling me it's a great day?" I looked directly into her eyes and said, "Yes, yes, you are having a great day!" I noticed something start to change in her. She straightened her posture, raised her chin, and relaxed her shoulders. I could see peace show on her face, and then she smiled. I knew then that she had gotten it! She realized that she alone gets to choose how she wants her day to be, and she decided in that moment to change her belief and have the day she wanted.

The next day, she called me, and she was so excited that I could feel her smile through the phone. The situation that she thought was causing her to have a bad day, had turned around and turned out even better than she hoped. She thanked me several times and asked me if I would coach her on how to develop a positive, faith-believing mindset that she could use to help her live the life she really wanted, instead of the way she was living then. I told her I would be honored to support her in developing the skills needed to be free from negative thoughts, and to learn how to tap into the power of faith so that she can have everything she wants in her life.

Working with her not only changed her life for the better, but it also changed my life too! I discovered that GOD has given me a calling to show women how to use faith instead of fear to reach the destiny that they've been searching for, with clarity and confidence. I love to help women grow stronger in their faith and belief so that they will never have to settle for less but will receive everything they desire in their lives. Check out how we can work together, at www.theinspiredwomanbook.com.

Chapter 3

This is Who I REALLY AM

"The LORD makes firm the steps of the one who delights in HIM; though she may stumble, she will not fall, for the LORD upholds her with HIS hand."
(Psalm 37:23-24)

I Am a Child of GOD

This is where the fun begins: your identity. Everybody thinks they know who they are. In the last chapter, I told you who you're not, and now you are going to learn the truth about who you really are.

This may surprise you, but a lot of what you have been told is not the truth. The truth shall make you free. Because we live in a fallen world, where lucifer controls the airways and the systems in society, lies are used to keep people in a mindset that serves his purpose and not GOD'S purpose. That is why I had to set a foundation first before I can take you into the deep, spiritual truths that I will be sharing with you now. But, before I go any further, let me share why identity is so important.

All throughout the Bible, GOD always started with identity before HE did the next thing HE was going to do. In Genesis, HE said, *"Let us make man in our image, after our likeness ..."* (Genesis 1:26 KJV). Here we see clearly that HE established identity as the foundation for mankind. This understanding of our identity as been seized and manipulated to what we currently see in the world today. Remember, GOD did not create the world; HE created the earth, and HE created the Kingdom.

You can look in the Bible concerning Abraham, Moses, the prophets, Peter, and more. They all went through a pattern of understanding who they really are in their identity. This is very important to GOD; therefore, it is important to us. Whatever GOD deems important, we must also acknowledge its importance.

I must go deeper with you into understanding who you are. Please give me some grace as I share this with you, as I know it may be hard to accept truth that is new to you. I thought I was to have written this book several years ago, about hearing GOD'S voice. I'm still going to do that, but I felt the leading of the LORD to go in a slightly different way.

Then when COVID-19 hit and the LORD started visiting me in my dreams and revealing the truth about what's really happening in the world, I had to be obedient and write in this book what HE wants me to share with you. HE wants me to share the knowledge and understanding about faith, because you will need it in abundance to withstand the delusions that will be released in the world soon. If you don't know the truth about who you really are, you may fall prey to the evil one and his devices that come only to kill, steal, and destroy. I don't want that to happen to you; that is why I must share this with you.

Let me tell you how I came to know who I really am. My first memory of GOD speaking to me was when I was four or five years old. My siblings and I were all watching the movie *The Ten Commandments,* during the Easter holiday. Back then, we only had a black and white TV, and the antenna was broken, so we had a hanger stuck in the location where the antenna used to be. When the movie got to the part where JESUS was carrying HIS cross, I was in tears; I was trying to hold them back, but I couldn't. Then, when they hammered the nails in HIS hands and feet, I jumped every time they struck the nail. As I watched them raise the cross with him on it, and the blood from his hands and feet falling, I couldn't take it any longer—it seemed as though I could feel all the pain HE was feeling. I still have this gift even today. I can feel certain people's pain. When I looked at that scene with HIM on that cross, I heard a voice in my ear tell me, "What you're seeing now is real; this did happen to me." I immediately asked my siblings, "Did you all hear that?" They looked at me like I was crazy! I knew then that something was different about me, but I didn't know what. There were many other times I had experiences where I couldn't understand why I was hearing and seeing things that others did not hear or see. Eventually, I stopped telling my family about it because they would talk bad about me and say I should be put in a crazy house. You know how siblings can be mean sometimes.

It wasn't until I gave my life to CHRIST that I finally received understanding of what was happening to me when I would hear this voice. GOD HIMSELF told me I was a prophet, and HE chose me from the beginning to hear HIS voice. I was in awe! HE even took me all the way back to when I was a baby and showed me what I had seen then—which, of course, I wouldn't remember unless someone showed me a picture or something. Well, that's what HE did. Wow! Our GOD is awesome! HE can do things that will blow your mind!

So, now that HE told me I was a prophet, HE proved it to me. I was in a church that didn't recognize women in the five-fold ministry, meaning women being apostles, prophets, evangelists, pastors, and teachers. One day after coming home from church, I asked the LORD about it, and HE immediately said, "Go to Luke 2:36 and read it." I had never read that verse before; I was just a babe in CHRIST, and this was the first time I had ever seen this scripture. The scripture said, *"And there was one Anna, a prophetess, the daughter of Phanuel, of the tribe of Asher: she was of a great age and had lived with her husband seven years from her virginity"* (KJV). It goes on to say how she ministered to the people in the temple. The LORD answered me immediately by showing me exactly where in the Word the truth was about women that HE chooses to serve HIM as HIS servant. I was set free! Never again can man tell me who I am—only GOD can tell me who I am.

This was just the first step to opening my mind so that I could hear the truth and know that my identity is in CHRIST. Now I'm ready and I'm hungry for more—my faith is high, I'm learning the truth, it's making sense, it's freeing my mind, and I'm going all the way in—and nothing will stop me now.

You must stay in Genesis, because there is so much truth to be found there. The world has put false information out into the educational system, and people are believing it so much that they now think there is no male and female but whatever you choose to call yourself. That is a lie from the pit of hell.

This is why you must stay strong in your faith and allow the power of GOD to lead and guide you into all truth, so that you will not fall into delusion and deception. You are thinking now, "Am I on the right path? Is what I'm feeling right now real?" If you asked that question right now, then you are on the right path. Your destiny is starting to reveal more and more to you. Don't be afraid; lean into it as we go deeper, and you will be free.

I Am a Partaker of HIS Divine Nature

There is a group of people in the United States and abroad, who have had their identity taken from them because they were shipped to a foreign land over 400 years ago. You know who I'm talking about. They call themselves by different names, like African American, Black, and others.

I no longer identify with these names because they are not true. Once your mind has been exposed to truth, you will no longer accept the lie. My prayer is that more of GOD'S people will receive the true revelation of GOD'S Word and begin to walk in freedom and truth.

Once again, we must go back to Genesis, and look at the land, the people, and the bloodline. When you put two and two together, there's only one answer. How did we miss it? We didn't. It was deliberately withheld from you, when they changed certain things, hid certain things, created other things, and manipulated a lot of things, so that their systems would do what they wanted them to do. Pure evil. I wouldn't be able to write all the things I now understand about the world's systems here, but I promise you I will give you enough to make your head spin and make you want to seek out more truth. As a prophet of GOD, every day, the Word of GOD reveals itself more and more to me, and sometimes I must hold my head in my hands to make it slow down.

One thing I know for sure is that GOD is in control; HE will always be in control, and HE is the only one who can create life. Everything else is counterfeit or a lie.

Have you ever asked yourself why this group of people were stripped of their heritage; why they don't know their true lineage? Everybody else in the world knows theirs, but this group does not. This deception is so big that they had to hide this group of people from their identity to work their system into this world they created. Wow! I'm blown away by that. This goes deep. I can't believe they would go to such depths to do this to a people, a nation.

It wasn't just any people or nation; it was GOD'S chosen people, the descendants of Abraham, Isaac, and Jacob. The Bible tells the stories of how GOD spoke to Abraham and told him that his descendants would be like the stars and the sand of the earth—so plentiful you wouldn't be able to count them. Then GOD told the prophets that because HIS chosen people had bowed down and worshiped false gods and sinned against GOD, they would be taken into captivity for 70 years in Babylon, and then 400 years of bondage in Egypt.

Look at these areas; look at the part of the world they are located in. These people were not the people we were told were GOD'S chosen people. Somebody did a switch on us to make us believe these people could survive in the heat of Egypt, work for 400 years, and have white skin.

That's not possible. I know you know this, but what I think you don't know is why it was done and who did it. Yes, yes, I know you know it was satan, but I'm talking about whose or what bloodline satan worked through to get this all done. Remember, lucifer, satan or whatever you want to call him, had an agenda from the moment he sinned against GOD, and he has been working that agenda ever since.

I Am a New Creature

"Now that you are born again, you are a new creature. The Bible says, "Therefore if any man be in CHRIST, he is a new creature; old things are passed away; behold, all things are become new."
(2 Corinthians 5:17 KJV).

I love this verse because it raises your belief and faith in GOD immediately. Whenever you see the word "BEHOLD" in a scripture, it's letting you know a dramatic change has taken place or will take place. It confirms that whatever was before, is now no longer.

What does it mean when you are a new creature in CHRIST? When you were born, you were born into the fallen state of sin. That means, the curse of Adam was your nature. CHRIST came to redeem us from the curse of sin, by dying on the cross.

Many people do not know HIM as LORD and SAVIOR; therefore, they live out their lives in sin. But when you ask GOD to save you, by repenting, getting baptized in HIS name, and receiving the gift of the HOLY SPIRIT, you are now born again and a new creature in CHRIST. This is where the old things pass away. You die from your sins, and you are born again and are a new creature in CHRIST.

That is why you feel different, look different, and act different, because you are new in CHRIST. You now have a new name—you are now reconciled back to your FATHER, your CREATOR. Your spirit has been reunited with the SPIRIT of GOD. They are now one.

Do you know what happens when you understand that you are now connected spiritually with GOD? You can feel HIM in your physical body, you can hear HIM in your spirit, you can ask HIM questions, and HE will answer you. This is life; this is life abundantly!

Knowing who you are is the most exhilarating knowledge you can learn about yourself. It's so freeing and exciting to know your earthly mind is now open to receive unlimited knowledge and revelations of truth.

This is what faith is. It's the connection with spiritual things that transcends your natural understanding, and because it's more real than what your natural eyes see, it manifests out of the spiritual into the natural. I get excited every time I think about it, because it raises my belief and trust in the ALMIGHTY GOD so much that I can't contain it. I feel it (faith) growing stronger and stronger, so much so that I just want to shout it out to the world! Do you feel it? Do you know how to magnify your faith?

In my coaching business, I have an exercise that I love to do with my clients, that shows them how to immediately feel faith moving in their physical bodies. Did you know you can feel faith moving? It feels great! One time, one of my clients couldn't stop crying because she felt so good. It made me start crying too! It was such a strong feeling of love and joy. We didn't want to come out of it.

I Am the Righteousness of GOD in CHRIST

The Bible tells us to *"seek first the Kingdom of GOD and HIS righteousness, and all these things shall be added unto you"* (Matthew 6:33 KJV). How do we know we are righteous? When we seek HIM and HIS kingdom.

The Kingdom of GOD is not the kingdom of this world. It has nothing in common with this world's systems. Everything operates in righteousness because the KING is righteous; therefore, HIS people are righteous. You must know and believe this in your heart, and when you do, you will start to see a change in everything you do. Your thoughts will change, your language will change, how you see and treat people will change, and you will do things differently.

It is in your knowing that you will start to live a righteous lifestyle. Righteousness just means doing the right things the way our LORD would do them. If we study GOD'S Word, we will learn what those right things are. Then we can apply them into our everyday situations and have success in those areas.

When we walk in righteousness, we gain favor. The favor of GOD shows up and blesses everything we do. It even passes down to our children and our families. You go on a job interview, and you thought they would offer you one salary, but they offer you 20k more. You take a test to get your certification in your field of study and you not only pass but you get a perfect score! These are proof that GOD has favored you in these areas. Can you think of a time when you thought you didn't do well, but when it was over, you did better than you thought you could ever do? That's favor working in your life.

I remember when I was studying to take my insurance license exam, and I was so scared. I felt like I wasn't ready. The exam was all computerized and we had to go into a controlled environment to ensure that no cheating could take place. When I went into the small booth where I was to take the exam, I saw the first question it asked me, and I froze. I didn't know the answer. All the questions were multiple choice, and I had no clue which one was the correct answer. Then I got to some answers I knew, but I still saw so many questions I didn't know. When I left that room, I felt defeated and very sad. I just knew I had failed because there were so many questions I did not know. After I grabbed my things and went out of the room, the facilitator came to me with a big smile on her face to tell me that I had passed! I couldn't believe it! I kept asking her, "Are you sure?" She said, "Yes!" Wow, not only did I pass, but I passed the health side of the test, and I never even studied the health side of the test! Wow! That was favor operating in my life even when I didn't know it.

Living righteously brings so many blessings into your life that you could never count them all. You must always remember that you are the righteousness in CHRIST, and for knowing this, you allow GOD'S favor to show up and bless you exceedingly and abundantly, more than you could ask for. *"For in the gospel the righteousness of GOD is revealed—a righteousness that is by faith from first to last, just as it is written: The righteous shall live by faith"* (Romans 1:16-17).

Chapter 4

I Can See Clearly Now the Rain is Gone

"For we walk by faith, not by sight."
(2 Corinthians 5:7)

Behold Old Things Have Passed Away

Remember back in your childhood, right around the age of 12 or 13, when you no longer wanted to play with your dolls? They somehow didn't give you the same joy and fun that you experienced when you were five and six—those same dolls that were given to you for Christmas or on your birthday, and all the excitement you felt opening the box and playing with them for the first time.

Now you're 13 and getting ready to go to middle school. New things are happening—new friends, new teachers, new clothes—everything is different. You look at your dolls and they now seem old. It seems like you've had them for a long time, and they're just sitting on your dresser, in a corner. You don't play with them anymore. It's as if they have passed away from your memories.

You have new memories now. That's how it is when you are born into the Kingdom. You start to notice that your thinking has changed; old ways of doing things no longer serve you. The old things you used to do don't feel the same.

It's like trying to put on a size 6 pair of jeans, when you know you are a size 10. They don't fit. No matter how hard you try, the size 6 doesn't fit. You have changed and you can't go back to the way it used to be. Old things have passed away.

The Bible says that you cannot put new wine in an old press, because if you do, the new wine will burst out from the old press. So now that old things have passed away, we must step into the new way. There is no other option. Our faith grows every day because we are new; old things have passed away: old thoughts, old beliefs, old actions, and old understandings.

Sometimes, we mourn for the things of the past. Our past can be comforting and take us back to a time in our lives when things were simple and easy, and we didn't have to worry about things. What happens is, we can get stuck in the old things, and that causes us not to invest the time and energy to bring change and help our future shine clear so that we can operate from a place of newness. When our faith is operating in a Kingdom mindset, we start to see so many new things; not only in our thoughts but in how we feel and where we're going and what's truly happening. Our faith can take us so many places and bring about change that causes us to create and learn and develop beautiful ways of expressing ourselves. The beauty of the gifts and talents that GOD has given us is so rewarding and fulfilling when we let go of all the old things—all the things that kept us bound and stuck. When we release our faith with newness of thought and understanding, revelation starts appearing and we start walking into territory that we never knew existed. It's so beautiful. It's so fulfilling. It's so rewarding. You may not be able to understand what is happening to you, but you know something is happening, because you're not the same. Behold, all things have become new! You are a new creature in CHRIST!

Faith Comes by Hearing

Did you hear that? Try again. Be still and lower your ear! No, not your physical ear—your spiritual ear!

If you didn't hear that, then how can you have faith? You say, "I don't know how to hear HIM." I would say, "Yes, you do." You just don't know how to recognize HIS voice from your natural inner voice or maybe the voice of the evil one too.

When you first gave your life to CHRIST, you were a babe in CHRIST. As you started noticing and experiencing the changes in your words, actions, decisions, and thoughts, you knew you were growing and changing in the things of GOD. It was easier to do the things you now know was the right things to do, but now that you are older, and more mature in CHRIST, things aren't as noticeable as they used to be.

The cares of this world have creeped in; you're so busy taking care of family, a household, a job, and a ministry, that you're never quiet and still long enough during your day to stop and listen and hear what GOD is saying to your spirit. Then your faith levels go down, and you don't recognize how low they are until you need them.

An example might be, you get a bad health report, and you need your faith to get through it, but because you haven't been listening to hear GOD'S Word regularly, instead of faith, you feel fear, and it rises upon you so high that you can't feel anything but the fear. This fear will keep you from releasing your faith, which is what you will need for healing to come into your body.

When our faith is high, because we're in the Word consistently every day, meditating on the Word night and day, the Bible says, *"Then ye shall have good success."* That means goodness and mercy shall follow you all the days long.

You already have what it takes to hear the HOLY SPIRIT speak to you every day. HE is speaking to you every day, giving you truth and guidance. All you must do is *"be still, and know that HE is GOD,"* and you will sharpen your spiritual ears and hear HIM more and more.

Visions of Truth

There was a song written by Johnny Nash, called, "I Can See Clearly Now the Rain Is Gone." I used to love this song because it gave me hope that after the rain, clarity would come, and I would make it to the other side and be happy. GOD wants us to see it before the rain. HE wants us to envision and believe the truth of HIS Word and what HE'S showing us we can do, be, and have.

There is only one truth. So many false truths have gone out into the world that sometimes we can't discern what is true and what is not true. When you have vision, added with your faith, you can see it happening for you. Truth shows up and it helps you to be able to recognize when the false shows up, because it doesn't line up with the vision that you have. Your vision is key; your vision will lead and guide you into all truth. Vision has depth, light, and energy. It produces and releases a vibration that goes out into the atmosphere and starts the process that GOD created to bring to life the thing you envisioned.

Don't let your vision die out. Keep it fresh, relevant, energized, and reverent. You wouldn't have this vision if GOD had not placed it inside of you.

Think right now about a vision or desire that you want to see happen in your life right now. Is it to start a business, to own a home, or to travel to some place warm? Now, take that vision and add lots of detail to it. Add colors, activities, friends, and family, and don't forget the fun! You didn't just think that up; it was given to you by the HOLY SPIRIT. When you are aligned with GOD, you are connected to the HOLY SPIRIT. HE is the vine, and you are the branch; therefore, everything in HIM flows into you. Now, when you write your vision down and make it plain and easy to understand, you have something to run with. Others can run with you as well.

Visions of truth are a gift from GOD. HE always wants you to see the truth, because HE is the truth. If HE shows you a vision, it's because it is true, and it shall come to pass if you believe and doubt not. *"Now faith is the substance of things hoped for, the evidence of things not seen"* (Hebrew 11:1 KJV).

I remember a vision I had of myself holding a microphone and speaking in front of a large crowd. In this vision, I was sharing my story. I felt the fear of walking out on the stage and looking out into the audience and seeing all the people's faces looking back at me with anticipation in their eyes, waiting for me to open my mouth and speak. The first couple of sentences were mumbled, with shaking lips and stuttering words, but as I started to take my mind off myself and think about the people GOD had entrusted me to share my story with, I realized that I was no longer afraid to speak. A boldness came upon me, and I spoke with courage and conviction; they could feel my heart and soul in every word I said. They smiled and cheered me on when I got to the victory of my testimony of healing and deliverance. It was as though I became one with my audience and we were blessing each other back and forth. It was so beautiful to see their faces light up with joy and excitement and their lives change also.

When you can feel your vision as if it is happening right now, that is when you know it is true and it will come to pass.

Well, that vision did come to pass just a few years later, and it happened just like I saw in the vision. Sometimes, you don't remember all the details until it happens, but then all the small details come flooding back into your memory and you are able to see everything you saw when you first had the vision.

GOD is true; HIS Word is true! If HE promised you something, then it will come to pass. Let your visions live, let your visions soar, and let your heart believe, no matter how long it takes for the vision to become real in your life.

"And the LORD answered me, and said, write the vision, and make it plain upon tables, that he may run that reads it. For the vision is yet for an appointed time, but at the end it shall speak, and not lie, though it tarry, wait for it; because it will surely come, it will not tarry."
(Habakkuk 2:2-3)

GOD Is Speaking to Me

Speak, LORD; speak! If you invite HIM to speak to you, HE will. HE created you because HE wanted to have a relationship with you. In the Book of Genesis, that was one of the first things HE did: HE spoke! Why would HE set the example and not want us to have it too?

When I was working for an insurance company, I won a free trip for myself and my husband to go on a 5-island cruise, leaving from Puerto Rico. It was such a beautiful trip. When we stopped at the port of the 3rd island of the trip, my husband didn't want to get off the ship, so I went by myself.

As I was walking along the shore, I saw a boardwalk up ahead that ran close to the water where the big rocks were located. I continued to walk so that I could walk on this boardwalk. After just a few steps in, I decided to stop and just take in the beautiful scenery and enjoy the fresh breeze on my face.

I looked all around me; it was such a beautiful sight. The sun was glistening off the water, the waves were rushing back and forth, and a cool breeze was blowing on my face. I closed my eyes to feel it deeply; I stood there in awe and joy, taking in all of GOD'S beauty. With a smile on my face, I just allowed the HOLY SPIRIT to fill me up more and more with love and joy of this experience. As I slowly opened my eyes and looked around one more time at all the splendor of beauty before me, I stopped and focused my eyes on the rocks. The big rocks were on both sides of me where I was standing. I saw the waves hitting them repeatedly. I just kept watching them as if I couldn't stop watching them. Then I heard the HOLY SPIRIT speak! I immediately recognized HIS voice. When you spend time with the LORD through prayer and reading HIS Word, you can't help but to get to know HIM and know HIM well. The Bible says, *"My sheep know my voice and I know them, and they follow me"* (John 10:27 KJV). I prepared myself in anticipation of hearing more of what HE would say to me. I stilled my thoughts; I humbled my heart so that nothing could hinder this time of communion. Then I heard HIM say, "See how the waves never stop hitting the rocks? That is how much I am always speaking to my people, but they are not hearing me." I was so grateful that HE was sharing HIS heart with me, that I just stood there in revert love and awe of the revelation that I had just heard. HE continued to share how HE wants to draw close to HIS people and talk with them daily, but they are so busy that they are not hearing HIS voice speak to them.

It was from this conversation that I am writing this book today. HE told me to "write the book." HE wanted me to encourage HIS people to know that HE wants to speak to them daily; HE wants to draw closer to them, and them closer to HIM. I will never forget that day! It changed my life. I knew without a shadow of a doubt that I had been hearing HIS voice every day since childhood, even though I didn't know it.

You can hear HIS voice every day. HE wants to talk with you and have a close relationship with you. It's not hard to do; it's easy! But first you must be born of the Water and the HOLY SPIRIT. These are your insurances or protection from evil forces infiltrating and disrupting the words you hear. Once you have these in place, you are now equipped to go and explore and learn everything you want, and the HOLY SPIRIT will tell you everything. Do you have a problem and you don't know what to do, or what your next step should be? Have a conversation with GOD and watch what happens next. You will see, hear, or do something that will solve your problem, all because you are allowing the HOLY SPIRIT to speak, and you hear HIS voice. I help women to do just that. When I coach my clients, I give them a blueprint to follow each day that will develop their ability to hear HIM with more clarity and frequency. Being chosen by GOD to serve HIS people, I love to see women's hearts open when they walk in a newness of hearing GOD every day, all day! I also have resources available for you. Just go to www.theinspiredwomanbook.com and pick them up.

In All Thy Getting, Get Understanding

What are you doing? You're so busy going here and there. Why are you doing that? You don't know; you're just reacting to whatever comes to mind. You think you're getting this; you think you're getting that, but the truth be told, you are just floundering, going around in circles, day after day, month after month, and year after year.

Now you see, you are on a hamster wheel, going around and around, going nowhere fast. You ask yourself the questions, "What do I really want? Why am I not where I thought I would be? I want this, I want that, and yet nothing is coming help!"

Where is your understanding? Where is your wisdom? You're doing everything except getting to understand. Think back to when you first started school. Everything was planned out for you: what you would learn in kindergarten, elementary school, and high school. You followed the whole plan without question. Everybody did—us, our parents, and our grandparents. Then we were told to go to college or learn a trade or get a job. Those were our options. Why? So that we could be useful to society. Notice how that still didn't explain the real reasons they planned out our first 18 years? Yes, they gave us the worldly reasons to follow their plans, but we didn't get GOD'S way to follow HIS plans for our lives—until we gave our lives to CHRIST and were born of HIS SPIRIT.

For the first time in your life, you were now receiving the truth. Without truth, there can be no understanding. With truth, there will be understanding. The Bible says, *"Wisdom is the principal thing; therefore, get wisdom, and with all thy getting, get understanding"* (Proverbs 4:7 KJV). Your true understanding comes from GOD. It comes from GOD'S Word. The Bible says, *"If any of you lack wisdom, let him ask of GOD, that give to all men liberally, and upbraided not; and it shall be given him."* I ask for wisdom, knowledge, and understanding every day. It's a non-negotiable for my everyday life. Even for the small simple things, I ask for wisdom, because the small things can turn into big things if I don't have the wisdom to ensure that I am doing the right thing and the best thing in that situation.

When you ask for wisdom and understanding, our FATHER will always give it to you. HE wants us to be wise and know that we can have success in every area of our lives. The fear of the LORD is the beginning of wisdom. Having this understanding as your foundation will keep you strong and prosperous. Your faith will be strong because you know that wisdom and understanding is always available to you when you need it. All you must do is ask for it.

So, what are you asking for today? Wisdom! It is one of the best tools GOD has given us that will never go away. GOD'S Word is our confirmation that wisdom will never go away! Use this tool every day. Learn more every day; receive everything you need from it every day, and you will see your life change dramatically.

Chapter 5

GOD Is Faithful

"For everyone born of GOD overcomes the world. This is the victory that has overcome the world, even our faith."
1 John 5:4

First You Have to Let Go and Forgive

Forgiveness is not for the person you are forgiving. Forgiveness is for you!

Everyone who lives on this Earth, one time or another during their lifetime, will have a situation where they must choose to either forgive or not to forgive. Unfortunately, we have this choice many times in our lifetime. It seems to get easier, but it really depends on the offense that was done and where you are in your mindset of understanding what forgiveness is and how to do it.

JESUS gave us many examples of how and why we must forgive. HE knew that this one thing could keep us bounded and sick for many years if we didn't fix it or make the right decisions concerning forgiveness. When we make the decision to forgive, and let that person know we have forgiven them, immediately everything changes for you. First, your body releases blockages, inflammation, and toxins out of your bloodstream. You will feel lighter, refreshed, and renewed. You will also start to feel your connection back to the SPIRIT of GOD.

Forgiveness not only sets you free, but it also sets the other person free. They are now able to receive forgiveness and all the blessing that comes from a forgiving heart. Don't hold on to unforgiveness in your heart. It will cause you much pain, physically, emotionally, and spiritually. The evil one tries to keep you in an unforgiving state of mind because he knows if you are there, he can wreak havoc on your life. The evil one only wants to kill, steal, and destroy everything that GOD has and wants for your life. Every time you say "I'm sorry" or "Will you forgive me?" the evil one must take his hands off you immediately. He has no right to torment you any further in this area. You will be set free from his hold on your mind—from what you were feeling about that person. You may not feel it all at once, but your mindset will change, and you will see the changes happening every day.

Believe with All Your Heart

Let's look at your heart. We're not talking about your physical heart but your spiritual heart. Science is continuing to confirm the truth of GOD'S Word more and more every day. Recently, they found a connection between the brain and the heart; that our experiences are in both places. Could this be why the Bible says, *"Keep thy heart with all diligence; for out of it are the issues of life"* (Proverbs 4:23 KJV). It also says, *"Trust in the LORD with all thine heart"* (Proverbs 3:5 KJV).

So, how do you believe with all your heart? First, you must surrender. You must surrender your will, the need to be right, to be in control, to do what you think or believe to be right, and acknowledge that there is only one truth, and that truth is GOD. Once you are clear and in agreement and aligned to GOD'S Word, then you can open your heart to receive and believe GOD with your whole heart. You will know you're there when you pray and start to feel emotions pulling on your heart, because a powerful flow of love will overtake you, and you might start crying tears of honor, joy, and adoration for HIM.

When your heart is open and you know that GOD only has good things for you, you can rest in HIM and let your knowing of truth reign in you and keep you in a spiritual state of believing only in HIM. Put nothing before that belief.

This brings to my memory a few years ago when I wanted to understand why I do the things that I do. I wanted to know why Cyndi is the person she is right now, and how she got there. One day as I was taking my daily walk, I felt GOD'S love come upon me like I've never felt before. HE was not only telling me how much HE loves me, but HE was showing me how much HE loves me by letting me have an experience where I could physically feel HIS love all over me and all around me. It was as if my eyes were opened for the very first time to see HIS love.

Have you ever had an experience like this? If not, you can. This is what our FATHER wants you to have. HE wants to pour out HIS love upon you like you've never experienced before. When HE does, you will never be the same. You will never doubt HIS love for you. Your faith will rise to a level you've only dreamed about. You can have this. It all starts with your belief. You must believe with all your heart.

Here's how to start: Close your eyes and take a deep breath three times. Repeat in your mind the words, "I know HE loves me; HE loves me so much. I love HIM with all my heart, and I know HE will always love me." You must mean it with truth and love. The more you let go and give into the truth that you know HE loves you, the more you will start to feel your emotions rise; you might even shed a tear or two, and that's good because now you know it's happening for you—you are feeling HIS love come upon you. The more you practice this exercise, the easier and more intense it will come.

Ask And It Shall Be Given

GOD'S Word tells us, in Matthew 7:7, *"Ask, and it shall be given you; seek, and ye shall find; knock, and it shall be opened unto you* (KJV).

YESHUA reveals a major secret of the Kingdom to us in this verse. You were taught to ask for things, abilities, and such, but it was always surface stuff, based on where you were in your life journey. When we were kids, we asked for toys; when we were teenagers, we asked for clothes or a car. Then when we became adults, we asked for bigger things, like homes, businesses, a husband, jobs, and more.

GOD wants us to go deeper. HE wants you to ask HIM for greater! HE wants you to ask HIM for spiritual things, like patience, long suffering, peace, wisdom, and joy. When you ask for these deeper things, you can go deeper and seek truth and more meaning in your life. When you ask, you will know what to look for and can go further in your search and find more. The more you search, the more you will find, and the deeper you will go into discovering more of what HE has for you. No one else can do this for you. You must desire and want to see more doors open to you. The more you search, the more you will find. Then when you find it, you will be ready to knock. Keep knocking until the doors open and you walk in and receive all that you asked for!

What are you asking GOD for? Is it surface level or is it Spirit level? Your FATHER wants to give you the desires of your heart. HE'S saying HE will give you good gifts. You can ask HIM for the simple things, but can you imagine what it would look like if you asked HIM for greater things, like HIS vision for your life, how to hear HIS voice, or how to walk in your gifts and see them manifest blessings in your life? There is so much HE wants to give you; HE'S just waiting for you to ask.

When I was a kid (I don't remember the exact age), I asked GOD for long hair. That was just something young girls did because their girlfriends at school had long hair and you wanted to look like your best friend who had long hair, so you thought that if you could just ask the FATHER for long hair, you would instantly get long hair. Well, that didn't happen in my childhood, but when I had my first child, I noticed my hair started growing. I didn't think much about it because I was taking care of life things, like home, career, finances, and more.

When I had my second daughter in my forties, I noticed that my hair was growing fast again. By this time, I was also seeing a lot of gray hair and I decided to stop perming and dying my hair. Well, one day I was combing my hair in the mirror, and I had the thought that I was going to cut my hair short and wear a short, curly, natural look. As soon as I finished that thought, I heard the LORD say to me, "You asked me for this hair and now you want to cut it?" I had to laugh because HE was right. I did ask for long hair as a child, but I never thought that I would have long hair at my age now! So, I told the LORD I wouldn't cut my hair because I did ask for it, even if it took 40 years to come.

If you ask GOD for something and it takes years to come, it's coming! Hold on; believe it no matter what! My hair is so long and gray now; I look forward to seeing how long HE's going to let it grow!

Trust GOD in all things, believe, and never stop. OUR GOD IS FAITHFUL! HIS promises are "yea and amen!" Ask always, trust, and believe always, and watch and see the LORD strong and mighty! HE will do it!

Pray Without Ceasing

A prayer can be one word long! Like, "Help." Don't let lack of time be an excuse not to pray. Prayer is our lifeline. It's our rock; it's our present and our future. It's the breath you breathe; it's the blood in your veins. You cannot live without it. The Bible says, *"Let everything that has breath praise the LORD."*

Imagine what will happen for you if you continually pray without ceasing. Would you be happier? Would you have more peace and joy? Your whole life would change and the lives of others around you too! There are times in our lives when prayer is so critical and needed that we can't even get one word out. You could be so devastated, or stricken with unbelief, that you go into shock; but GOD is so good that HE will send a prayer warrior to intercede on your behalf, and then deliverance and healing will show up and change everything. GOD knows what you need even before you know what you need. HE always makes a way of escape in times of trouble. Praying without cease is one of our secret weapons. It's always there for you to use whenever you need it.

I stopped going to church when I was twelve. I stopped praying and asking GOD for guidance. I went on with my life doing whatever I thought I was big enough to do. I made decisions that landed me in bad situations that led to stress and lots of turmoil. It wasn't until I was about to go to jail that I realized that I needed to pray and ask YESHUA to help me. In that one moment, I knew if I didn't pray and ask GOD to help me, my life would never be the same. Did I know what the outcome would be? No, but one thing I did know was that HE alone was the only one who could keep me from going to jail. I prayed like my life depended on it, because it did. I prayed with all I had, a sincere prayer of need. What I didn't know then, but I know now, is that I had faith the size of a mustard seed. GOD had given me faith to believe that HE would deliver me from the hands of evil.

You want to talk about a miracle? I saw a miracle that day. By the world's terms, I should have been locked up. I should have been in prison for many years, but GOD said, "Not so." When that police officer returned to my car and let me go, I knew it was only because of GOD'S grace that I was free; I was free to go. I give all praise and honor to my LORD and Savior every day when I think back to how HE delivered me from the hands of the evil one.

Pray, pray, and never stop praying. Even when everything is going well, keep praying. Pray over everything in your life—your home, your family and friends, your children and your marriage, your business, your bank account, your finances, your future—everything. Then watch and see how the blessings keep coming in every area of your life.

YESHUA gave us an example of how to pray, in Matthew 6:9-13 and Luke 11:2-4. Whenever you see something in the Bible mentioned more than one time, it is letting you know it's important and it's established by more than one witness.

Trust in the LORD Always

Proverbs 3:5 says, *"Trust in the LORD with all thine heart; and lean not unto thine own understanding"* (KJV).

I believe this is one of the areas where we are challenged the most: trusting GOD always. Every day, we have before us the concerns, issues, and challenges of life to deal with, and sometimes, those challenges cause us to worry and doubt that things will be okay. This isn't where GOD wants you to be. HE wants you to know beyond a shadow of a doubt that HE will take care of you, and everything will work out for your good. This takes practice and commitment to building your faith; to trust and believe even when it doesn't look like it will work out in your favor.

I am reminded of a time when my house was in foreclosure. It was the Friday before Labor Day weekend that a letter came in our mailbox, letting us know our house was scheduled to be sold at auction at the County Court House on the following Friday. I was so scared to lose my house. My husband and I didn't have the money to pay the six months of back mortgage payments we owed. Every week prior, for about 3 months, I had been receiving letters in my mailbox, trying to warn me not to let my house be foreclosed on without acting against it. I saved all the letters, never opening them but just putting them in a pile, not being sure what I would do with them. Some of these letters talked about wanting to buy my house, pennies on the dollar, or they could stop the foreclosure if we did XYZ. I didn't know these people; I didn't know if they were scammers or opportunists that would trick us out of our home. I had never had a home before, so I had never gone through something like this before.

Because it was Labor Day weekend, we couldn't talk to anyone that could possibly help us. We had to wait until Tuesday of the same week the auction was scheduled to take place. I was so sad, heartbroken, and defeated. I was so depressed that I couldn't get out of bed. The stress of the situation caused pain to take over my whole body. I shut down; I couldn't function for 3 days.

Then, when Tuesday came, I got up early and started praying. A boldness came upon me, like I've never felt before. My prayers were fierce and strong. I told satan, "You can't have my house!" As I was praying, I happened to glance at a picture of my father on the mantle by the fireplace, and I felt something happen inside of me that I can't explain. It was as if I was strong enough to pick up a car from off the road. I felt my body receive supernatural strength. The reason I believe this strength came upon me is because, the day when we met with the builders to put the contract in to have our house built, which was one of the happiest days of my life, when I got home that afternoon, around 4 p.m., the phone rang, letting me know that my father had just been killed by someone who had stolen a car and had ran a red light trying to outrun the police. He t-boned my father when he was trying to make a left turn. My father died on impact when his car landed after being airborne, because the driver of the stolen car had been driving over 100 miles an hour. That driver got out of his car with only a scratch on his head.

Glancing at the picture of my father, reminded me of that day and brought back all the emotions I felt when we put the contract in to have our beautiful home built. I knew then that I had to fight for my home, that I could not give up, and that I must do whatever it took to keep my home, and trust GOD for the rest!

Grow Strong in the Truth of the Word

When I finished praying and seeking GOD for guidance and direction, I went down into my office and grabbed the stack of letters that I had been collecting. I set them in the middle of my desk and just closed my eyes and said, "LORD, please let whoever answers the phone be able to help us." I opened the first letter and read a portion of it until I found a contact number. I called the number, but there was no answer. I picked up the second letter, and the same thing happened: there was no answer. This happened for about the first 7 to 8 letters: no one answered the phone. It was a little early, around 8:30 or so, but I needed help ASAP; I couldn't wait until later, so I continued to open and dial numbers. I wasn't going to stop until I found someone who could help us.

After opening about 7 or 8 letters, the very next letter I opened, a young man said, "Hello." My heart leaped with anticipation. I was so happy when he spoke; I felt hope rise in me. I had just prayed that whoever answered my call would be the one to help me, and bless GOD, it was true!

This young man wasn't just any man; he was a powerful man of GOD who loves the LORD, who knows his calling and uses his gifts and talents to bless the Body of CHRIST to buy and sell people's homes. When he told me who he was and why he was doing what he does, I knew GOD had sent this man to us. A peace came over me, the peace of GOD, which passed all my understanding. This peace I received doesn't come from the world but from GOD only.

When I told him about our situation, that our home was in foreclosure and scheduled to be sold at the County Court House this coming Friday, he immediately said the words I wanted and needed to hear. He said, "Mrs. Greene, don't worry, everything will be alright. I know exactly what needs to be done, and your home will not be sold at auction this Friday!" He assured me that what we needed to do next would clear our property from the docket in the court room and set in motion the plan to get our home out of foreclosure.

By the end of the day, we had our plan; we knew exactly what to do, and we started on the exact steps he told us to do. By Thursday morning, everything was done! We were praising GOD and singing songs of joy! We saw the hand of GOD move on our behalf and bless us exceedingly and abundantly above all that we could ask or think.

When I awoke up on Friday morning, I felt as if I was born again! I was refreshed, renewed, and filled with faith, because I knew my trust in GOD was real and strong. We are still in our beautiful home today, and I thank HIM every day for blessing us for this miracle HE gave us.

You can trust GOD above every circumstance you may be experiencing right now. You can trust HIM for the small things and the large things. You can trust HIM for healing, deliverance, finances—everything in your life—you can trust HIM to help you and bless you. HE is no respecter of any one person—what HE does for one, HE can do for everyone. I am a living testimony of the great things our FATHER can do! You will have a testimony too!

Chapter 6

Walk It Out, Speak It Out

"But those who hope in the LORD will renew their strength. They will soar on wings like eagles; they will run and not grow weary; they will walk and not be faint."
(Isaiah 40:31)

Are You Speaking Life or Death?

You are wonderful and fearfully made. Your FATHER breathed the breath of life into you. HE created everything you need to sustain life here on Earth. Nothing broken, nothing missing. HE created you in HIS image. HE gave you a mind and a will, so that you can choose what kind of life you want to live.

What are you choosing? Are you living in your past or are you praising HIM in your now? Where are your thoughts? Are they negative or are they positive? The Bible says, *"... out of the abundance of the heart, the mouth speaks"* (Matthew 12:34 KJV). What is coming from your heart? In Proverbs, the Bible says, *"Keep thy heart with all diligence; for out of it are the issues of life"* (Proverbs 4:23 KJV).

It is time to build your faith, and walk and talk only faith-filled words. Speak words that bring forth life into your heart. Your words have power; your words are containers that carry your faith and bring to you what you believe in your heart. If you believe you are ugly in your heart, you will look in the mirror and say to yourself, "I am ugly." Once said, you will now only see what you just said. You won't see that GOD made you fearfully and wonderfully. You won't see that HE said, *"You're the apple of my eye, and I love you, because you are my creation."*

Every time you speak death-filled words, the evil one is right there waiting to take those words and use them against you. If you say, "I am broke," guess what? You have just set in motion for those words to become a reality in your life. You are financially where you are today because of the words you spoke yesterday. You have angels all around you; their only job is to listen to your words to see if they are faith-filled words so that they can go and bring those things into your life, because they can see that you believe it in your heart. Angels cannot deliver your gifts when your word stops the train from moving forward. GOD is waiting on you so that HE can pour out blessings—lots of blessings—so much that you shall not have room to receive them all. HE wants you to speak life. HE'S crying out to you. HE'S sending hints, words, people, signs...

whatever HE can to get your attention so that you will change your words and HE can bless you abundantly!

"Well, you say, "how do I change my words?" It starts with a decision. First, recognize you have a word problem. Until you do this, you will not be able to move forward. Pray and ask GOD to help you recognize when you are speaking words that will hinder your faith and belief. Ask for wisdom before you say and do things, and you will receive it. Now you are ready to move into what I call the "Operation Faith Zone!"

Operation Faith Zone is where you go all in, take no prisoners, and be bold and on fire to speak power words every day in everything that you say and do. You will eat, sleep, and drink power faith words consistently and diligently every day. It will be so powerful that you couldn't stop it if you tried. These words will be words given to you by the HOLY SPIRIT for each situation you are in. These words will line up with and were also spoken by YESHUA, because they are life-giving and faith-filled. They will create much fruit in your life and change you and your surroundings.

When I coach my clients and give them a customized blueprint just for their "Operation Faith Zone," I see the transformation in their lives within just days of using the system. They start to have clarity about their career goals, and on how to bring back the sparkle in their marriages.

They find a new purpose that opens their understanding and gives them direction on how to get there. Their businesses would triple in revenue from the previous year. I've seen so many changes in my clients that I get so excited when a new client joins my coaching program, because I know they are going to explode with clarity and abundance in their life. If you would like more information about my programs, go to www.theinspiredwomanbook.com and get my free blueprint for the Operation Faith Zone now.

No Faith? Dead Work

Faith without works is dead. It has no life; therefore, it will bring forth no fruit. This book wants to show you how to use faith and receive everything you want in life. For that to take place, there are things that first must be agreed upon and understood.

First, you must know your identity, who you are in CHRIST. Second, you must be born of the Water and the SPIRIT. When you have these foundational truths in place, you are ready to move forward. The Bible says, *"Now faith is the substance of things hoped for, the evidence of things not seen"* (Hebrews 11:1 KJV). We already stated from the Bible that *"if you have faith as small as a mustard seed, you can say to the mountain, be thou removed and cast into the sea."* The LORD is letting you know how to operate using your faith. HE also says, *"Without faith, it is impossible to please HIM."*

Let's start with the word "now." So many people quote this scripture but leave out applying this one word in their actions. Now means now! Not yesterday, not tomorrow, but right now, this very second. This is key. Are you in faith right now? If not, it's dead faith. Moving on from the word "now," let's look at the word "faith." Do you understand what faith is? The world defines faith as complete trust or confidence in someone or something. We know it is more than that. It is relationship with our FATHER, who is our creator, and by faith, we know HE is a rewarder to those that diligently seek HIM. As you seek HIM and have a relationship, your faith is established in HIM. This is your evidence, your proof, that you already have what you say and believe you have.

When I put the contract in to have our house built, I had no money saved up for a down payment. To put the contract in, I had to find $1000 just to do that part. I've been in Sales all my life, so I got on the phone, and in 3 days, I sold $1000 of my products and went and signed the contract. A few days later, my sister asked me, "Cyndi, how much money do you have saved up to build your house?" I told her, "I don't have any money saved up." She said, "Then how are you going to build a house if you don't have any money saved up for it?" All I could say to her, with much boldness and conviction in my heart, was, "I don't know, but I'm building this house!" My belief and faith were so strong that even now I just thank GOD for giving me the faith and the words to speak life over that situation, instead of doubt and fear.

You must always, no matter the circumstance, no matter the "how," speak faith that is alive. Speak faith of what you want, not what you see or currently have. This is the substance that will bring it out of the unseen and into the now seen.

You can do it. You've already done it. You just stay the course; don't speak against it by speaking negative words about it. Keep your faith alive, live in faith daily, and tell yourself, "I believe, and I trust GOD; it's already done." Then give GOD praise every time it comes to your mind. Take a moment and just say, "Thank you, LORD." You will be amazed at how fast everything in your life will turn around for your good.

Be a Faithful Follower

Because you know these things about your faith, you are going to follow faith every day. You will be faithful and let your faith grow and grow. The Bible says, *"So then faith comes by hearing, and hearing by the Word of GOD"*

(Romans 10:17 KJV). You can hear GOD in anything. You can hear HIM in your daily walk, on a sign that's on the back of a car in front of you, in a movie, or hearing your own self speaking to someone. It could be a tree, off to the side of you that stands out from the rest. There are so many ways this can happen and when it does happen, it is amazing! The light comes on so bright, you couldn't miss it if you tried. When you hear HIM this way, through things and signs, they are there to keep you motivated, strong, and encouraged to stay faithful. They are there to keep you from giving up, to keep you going, and to let you know all is well. Best of all, they are there to let you know that you can do it!

One of the ways I follow faith every day is to look and expect GOD to speak to me through something or someone. I wake up with a mindset that "today I will receive all that GOD has for me." Then as I am going about my day, I watch and I look at any and everything that might be HIM speaking to me. HE never disappoints. HE always comes through, because I already know HE wants to speak to me every day, and all I must do is be open and believe in faith that it will happen for me today.

One day I was outside, and I saw a red cardinal in a tree. He was so pretty and bright that I couldn't take my eyes off him. Then I heard HOLY SPIRIT say, "That's me; I'm reminding you how much I love you!" It was so clear; I felt the warmth of HIS love come down on me. I cried because it was so real, and now I can't wait to see another red cardinal!

Walk By Faith, Your Steps Are Ordered

Keep moving; don't stop! You're on your path that GOD created just for you! Every step you take keeps you connected to your destiny, and your path will get only you there. There will be times when you will see a fork in the road, and you may stop and look left and then right, and then ask, "Which way should I go now?" That's normal. It's okay to ask, because the Bible says, *"Ask and it shall be given..."* (Matthew 7:7 KJV). Because you are walking in faith, you will be quiet and will sit still for just a moment, and then you will feel your spirit nudging you to step forward, and as you take the first step, and the next, it will get easier. Now your confidence will rise and you will move at a steady pace.

You will find yourself being guided in the direction that GOD wants you to take. It will feel right; it will feel peaceful. If it doesn't and you feel uncomfortable, then that is the HOLY SPIRIT signaling to you to turn around and go in the other direction. You will know without a doubt when you get this signal, because it will not let you rest until you turn around.

I am reminded of a time when I went on a job interview to work at a Christian high school. The interview went well. At the end of the interview, the lady offered me the job and said, "I would like to offer you the job at this pay rate." I thought about it for a couple of minutes. As I was processing whether that salary would work for me, I told her, "No, I'm sorry, I wouldn't be able to accept the position at that salary." She immediately said, "Will you accept it if I raise it by 10K more?" Just as I started to say no, the HOLY SPIRIT started jumping inside of me: "Take it, take it!" It wouldn't let me say no! I listened to the HOLY SPIRIT, and I said yes and accepted the position. The peace of GOD came upon me, and I knew right then and there that I had made the right decision to accept the job.

The HOLY SPIRIT would not let me take the wrong path. HE corrected me before the opportunity was gone. I didn't know my steps were ordered until I was about to step off the path that GOD had ordained for me to be on.

It's the same way for you. You may not recognize that your steps were ordered, until you step in the wrong direction and the HOLY SPIRIT keeps nudging you back on course. Don't you love this about our FATHER? HE knows exactly what we need and when we need it!

Observe and Do All

Obedience is better than sacrifice. How many times have you heard this? We were brought up to obey our parents, obey our elders, and anyone with authority over us. It's not until we mature a little more, or we go through something hard, that we really understand the deeper meaning of this. We all go through our teenage years, where we want to rebel against authority, so we set out to explore and make our own decisions, usually different than what our parents tell us. We step out into the world, saying, "I am going to do it my way," only to find out that what our moms said was true! We hated that she was right, so next time, we think, "I'm going to prove her wrong." We spent so much time focusing on the wrong things, that we didn't pay attention to the right things; things like looking and observing our surroundings, our actions, and our decisions to see if we are making the right decisions and what the true outcomes of those decisions are. Sometimes, we do things but they may not have been the best things to do in that situation, and we find out later that there was a better, easier way to do the thing that was done.

Sometimes, it's better to sit back and observe the full picture before you dive in. Moving too fast can cause more damage than waiting a few hours or days.

Know this, my sister: GOD will always have a path that will lead to truth. When you find that path and observe, study, access, and learn, you will do all that the HOLY SPIRIT is leading you to do. You will have success. HE'S not telling you to do something HE hasn't already given you the grace to complete. HE'S given you everything that pertains to life. HE wants you to live and live abundantly.

Cast Down Vain Imaginations

What are vain imaginations? Vain imaginations are thoughts or idea's that are contrary to the Word of GOD. These thoughts or ideals cause one to stray away from the truth of GOD'S Word, which then can lead you down a path of destruction.

GOD wants us to immediately pull down those thoughts out of our minds before they can take root and build a stronghold or worsen in our lives. There are many vain imaginations that can cross your mind on a given day; you are constantly being bombarded by signs and signals in your eye gate that we see around us, and our ear gate that we hear around us. The Bible says, *"Pray without ceasing."* The LORD knows we need this, because without it, we can be pulled into a darkness we never wanted to be in. You must always protect your heart and mind.

In the Book of Ephesians, Chapter 6:11 tells us to *"put on the whole armor of GOD, that ye may be able to stand against the wiles of the devil* (KJV)." Every piece of the armor will protect you and help you keep vain imaginations from infiltrating your heart to kill, steal, and destroy you.

Let's start with the helmet of salvation. When you accepted YESHUA as your LORD and Savior, you were born into the Body of CHRIST. Being a part of the Body, you now must prepare yourself daily with the tools GOD has given you. These tools will cause you to stand in victory every day. You are in a battle every day. Satan wants your mind, but by putting on the helmet of salvation, he cannot do a sneak attack into your thoughts and beliefs. You are covered; you are protected. He will try to put damaging thoughts into your mind that are contrary to GODS' Word, but it will not prosper, because you already know you have your helmet of salvation on; by faith, you know and believe it is so, and therefore you cannot fall into his evil devices.

When you do have a thought that doesn't line up with the Word of GOD, you will immediately reject it and say the opposite of that thought, to train your spirit to block out negative thoughts and replace them with positive thoughts that align with GOD'S Word. By continuing to diligently work on and manage your thoughts, it will become a lot easier, and you will see results faster.

Chapter 7

Plant a Seed and Watch It Grow

"The LORD is far from the wicked;
but HE heareth the prayer of the righteous."
(Proverbs 15:29)

Prayers of the Righteous

Every time you pray, you plant a seed. You always want your seed to be planted in good soil. Sometimes, your seed will fall on good ground; sometimes, it will fall on shallow ground, and sometimes, it will fall on stony ground. No matter what kind of ground it falls on, you must never stop planting that seed, because one day that seed will grow and bring forth a mighty harvest.

The Bible talks about how the LORD gives seed to the Sower. HE gives some 30, some 60, and some 100-fold. What makes your seed become 30, 60, or 100-fold? It's your faith. *"... If ye have faith as small as a grain of mustard seed, you can say to this mountain, be thy removed and it shall obey you and nothing shall be impossible unto you"* (Matthew 17:20 KJV).

A mustard seed is one of the smallest seeds known to man, yet it grows larger than you can imagine. YESHUA is making a point of visual context so that you can see that all you need is a little, and it will yield more than you comprehend that it can.

The Bible says, *"The effectual fervent prayer of a righteous man (woman) avails much"* (James 5:16 KJV). When we are in right standing with GOD, and we keep HIS commandments, we will love our neighbor as we love ourselves. Our prayers will land on good soil. Our hearts will be honest and sincere. We will humble ourselves and yield to the HOLY SPIRIT. We will be open to receive because we trust and believe GOD. This is where "100 fold" resides. This is where good fruit and big harvests manifest in your circumstances. You will experience more than you asked for. It comes so easy, with no sorrow or confusion. You will receive it, and you will be grateful for it.

As I said in a previous chapter, I grew up in the country, in a very small town, in Michigan. Being from a large family, we had to have a garden to offset the price of feeding so many people in our family. At a young age, I learned how to plant vegetables. Before you can put the seed in the ground, you must prepare the ground. First, it must be in a place that has good soil and sunlight. You wouldn't pick a place that is rocky and filled with stones. You would pick a place that is level and has soil that is fertile to grow things.

Once you have your spot and you know it is good for growing your food, it is time to clear away all the weeds, debris, sticks, and anything else that's in the way. Now it's time to till the land, which means to loosen the soil, or turn it over, so that the seeds will have a better chance of germinating into the soil and the roots will start to form.

Next, depending on what you're going to plant, you will make small holes down a row, making sure to separate each hole a certain distance from the next. Then it will be time to drop the seed into the holes for each row and cover them completely with the soil that is around the hole. Of course, you will need to water each row of your garden and make sure everything is okay.

If everything is done correctly, and the garden gets proper water and sunlight, you will start to see the sprouting of your new plants as they break through the ground. Oh, what a beautiful sight when you see all your hard work pay off and your plants are growing and on their way to producing what GOD created them to produce.

This is how your prayers work. Every time you pray, you are planting seeds that will grow in good ground. This ground will yield some 30, some 60, and some 100-fold returns in harvest to you. The more you plant, the more you will receive. That is why we should never stop praying. The Bible tells us to *"pray without ceasing."*

Don't Just Ask, Believe

"I believe, I believe, I believe...," but do you really believe? It's so easy to say but harder to do. Every day, we ask our FATHER for this or that, and then we say, "I believe I'm going to do XYZ," but deep inside, we still have doubt. That's not belief; that's being double-minded.

To know if you truly believe, you must be tested. You can even test yourself so that you will know if you're fooling yourself or if you really believe like you said you do. Sometimes, you will be tested even when you don't know you are being tested. I like this one the best, especially if I passed it! Giving an example, let's say you are believing GOD for a new job. You've prayed, you've asked HIM, and now the seed is planted, and you're waiting for the harvest to manifest. Every day, you wake up excited and eager to hear your phone ring, with someone asking you to come in for an interview. You go on the interview, and it goes very well in your eyes; so well that you know they are going to call you back and say, "You've got the job!"

Well, three days go by, then seven days, then two weeks, and you haven't heard anything from them. Now you're starting to get discouraged; your excitement has faded. You start doubting yourself and your abilities to do that job. Lastly, now you are speaking your negative thoughts out loud. You just flunked the test! Because you didn't pass the test, you will have to take it again.

So, you go on another interview, and you do the same thing; you leave and are feeling very positive they will offer you the job. But this time, you do things differently. Instead of waiting and filling your head with doubt and negative thoughts, you water your seed by thinking good thoughts and speaking positive words out loud, such as, "When I start this job, I will do XYZ." Then, when you least expect it, your phone will ring, and good news will follow. You have passed the test! You have applied Kingdom spiritual truth to your natural operations, which brought you success!

Faith is the soil; belief is the water! The more you plant and water, the more harvest you will receive!

It's time to go deeper into your faith. It's time to believe more and plant more seeds! You have been given everything you need—all the tools—now it's time to do the work. Study, learn, and apply, and you shall have good success. I believe in you; I know you can do it! I love helping my clients discover how strong they are, and how they already have everything inside of them to succeed.

You Will Bear Much Fruit

In Genesis, Chapter one, verse 28, GOD said, *"Be fruitful and multiply, and replenish the earth...."*

Many teach this verse to say that people should have many babies, who will also have babies. But I want you to look at this verse and go deeper into the revelation of GOD'S Word.

We know in this same Book, that GOD said a thing, and it was created. When HE said, "Let us make man in our image, after our likeness," HE wanted us to know that everything that is in HIM is also in us. Because we are HIS creation, HE wanted us to know we can create too!

So, when we know our identity, which is knowing who created us, we can operate in ways just like our Creator did.

YESHUA said, *"Ye shall know them by their fruits"* (Matthew 7:16 KJV). So, the question becomes, what kind of fruit are you producing? *"You will bear much fruit"* is not only talking about offspring; it also includes everything else you are creating.

When you're at work, and you're given a title and a job description, your employer is expecting to see fruit that produces the work listed in the job description and duties. You will be evaluated based on whether you produce what they paid you for over the course of that year.

In our faith walk with GOD, HE has spoken many things to us that HE desires us to learn and do. HE wants us to create and be fruitful and multiply whatever we put our hands to.

You have a natural gift, given to you by GOD to create whatever your heart is telling you to create. When you create, it's like putting a seed in the ground, and in time, it will produce a harvest. When it does, you will see and receive all the fruit from what you created. You have many, many gifts. When a child is born, a parent can watch their child play and discover their child's natural gifts. If the parent nurtures those gifts that they see in their child as she grows, that child may have a fulfilling career in that area, all because her parents saw her gifts at a young age and invested time and energy for that child's gift to grow.

This is how GOD created us. It's in our nature to create, to discover our gifts and talents and use them to be fruitful and multiply. You are fruitful; you can multiply anything your heart desires. When you do, you are showing the world GOD'S grace on your life. You are letting your light shine, and when others see you, they see the glory of GOD in your life. Doesn't that feel good?

All Things Are Possible

Believe, believe, and never stop believing in GOD. Never stop believing in what GOD has for you and what GOD has said about you. Always believe in yourself.

The enemy comes to kill, steal, and destroy. YESHUA said, *"I am come that they might have life, and that they might have it more abundantly"* (John 10:10 KJV). Without faith, it is impossible to believe that HE is a rewarder of them that diligently seek HIM. *"ALL things are possible to them who believe."*

When you trust and believe GOD for everything, HE promises that HIS Word will do that which it was sent to do. There is nothing GOD can't do. HE can do anything. The more you believe this, the more it will be true in your life. People want to see miracles every day. They won't believe something until they see it with their own eyes. But GOD wants you to trust and believe before you see it with your natural eyes. HE wants you to know it is possible and already done before you see it with your natural eyes.

All means ALL! Not some, not maybe, but ALL! Even when the report from the doctor says one thing but GOD says another, it's still possible! When the bill says one thing and your bank account says another, it's still possible. All things are possible to those that believe. You must believe; don't stop believing. Do whatever you have to do to keep your belief alive. Talk to yourself every day. Say positive affirmations out loud. Quote scriptures, read books, sing, scream... whatever it takes to keep you in belief mode.

Keep repeating, "All things are possible if I keep believing!" Say it every day, everywhere you go. Write it out on paper, put it on your refrigerator, your bathroom mirror, your car—put it everywhere!

When it becomes second nature to you, you will feel it all over you. You will eat, live, and breathe it! Nothing can stop you from receiving the possible! You can go to www.theinspiredwomanbook.com to get the blueprint for Operation Faith Zone.

Praying in the Spirit

Prayer changes everything. It is an offensive weapon that the evil one cannot win against. Every time you pray, you bring heaven down to Earth on your behalf. The more you pray, the more you are connected to our heavenly FATHER. The Bible tells us to *"pray without ceasing"* (1 Thessalonians 5:17 KJV). Prayer is how we communicate with our FATHER daily. This is how we praise HIM, worship HIM, and learn from HIM. HE loves us so much; HE wants to commune with us every day through prayer. There are different types of prayer, but all lead to the same place: talking with GOD and letting HIM into our lives, to lead and guide us through our life journey.

I want to talk about one type of prayer, called "praying in the SPIRIT." You may have heard about praying in the SPIRIT and what it is and how it is different than praying in your natural language you were born with. But I want you to know how powerful it is when you pray in the Spirit daily.

When you gave your life to CHRIST and received the gift of the HOLY SPIRIT, evident by speaking in tongues as the SPIRIT gave the utterance, that was the first day proving your connection back to the FATHER, with you now having direct communication with HIM in the SPIRIT. This communication between you and the HOLY SPIRIT keeps the evil one from accessing your words to try to steal what you are believing GOD for. Praying in your heavenly language grows and deepens your spiritual connection with the ALMIGHTY.

Maybe, as of reading this book, you have never been filled with the HOLY SPIRIT: speaking in tongues as the SPIRIT gives the utterance. If that is you, I want to take this time to invite you to know that this is available to you right now! Start by confessing to YESHUA that you know that you are a sinner, and that you are asking forgiveness for your sins, and then continue to pray and ask GOD to fill you with the HOLY SPIRIT right now, and then open your mouth and start to speak. You will notice sounds coming from your mouth that you don't understand, but GOD does, because HE is talking through you and to you. Oh, what a glorious day you will have when HE finishes filling you up with HIS SPIRIT! If it doesn't happen right away, don't give up; just continue to give HIM praise with a sincere heart, and it will come!

Do you remember the day you were filled with the HOLY SPIRIT and spoke in tongues for the very first time?

How did you feel afterwards? How did you feel the next day? Was it a life-changing event for you? It certainly was for me! I spoke in tongues all night long. When I awoke the next day, I still couldn't stop speaking. I saw the world as if it was new and I had never seen it before. I remember going outside and looking around as if I had never seen trees before. They looked greener and brighter than I remembered from the day before. I heard the birds chirping, and it sounded like music to my ears. The sky looked blue and clear; it was so beautiful. But the number one thing I remember is how I felt. I was so happy; I couldn't stop smiling. I had the joy of the LORD in me, and I felt it for the very first time. I smiled all day. My shoulders felt light as a feather. No one, even now, can tell me GOD isn't real. What I felt the morning after being born again and filled with HIS SPIRIT, no one can take away from me. I am sealed until the day of redemption, and you are too!

When you pray in the SPIRIT, you are building up your most holy faith—you are spending time and connecting with your CREATOR, your FATHER, your LORD and KING. This is what separates our GOD from all false religions. Our GOD is alive! And HE lives inside of us! Speaking in your heavenly language is proof that HE'S alive in you.

There are gifts that the FATHER has given to the Body of CHRIST, and one is the gift of tongues. This is not what I'm talking about here. Being filled with the HOLY SPIRIT as the SPIRIT of GOD gives the utterance, is for every believer.

Everyone who is born of the Water and the SPIRIT can speak in tongues, as the SPIRIT gives the utterance. It is a gift, and it's for everyone to receive.

Praying in the SPIRIT has power—power to heal the sick, cast out demons, raise the dead, and more! When you pray in the SPIRIT, demons run! They don't want to be anywhere around you. The Bible says, *"How should one chase a thousand, and two put ten thousand to flight..."* (Deuteronomy 32:30 KJV). Using this weapon can save and keep you safe from all hurt, danger, and harm. Pray daily; let your prayer life be a non-negotiable in your life. Don't let anyone or anything pull you away from the time you spend in prayer. Prayer can save your life! Prayer can save your family, your home, your marriage, your business... it can save everything! Never stop!

Pure Heart Knows It's the Window to Your Soul

One thing I know about seeds is that they are pure. When you plant an apple seed and it grows to a full-sized tree, you will see only apples on it. It started as a seed, and now it's producing apples after its kind. It is pure. It wasn't an orange seed or a pear seed or a grape seed; it was purely an apple seed and it created exactly what it was created to produce.

What is a pure heart? Is your heart pure? How does one obtain a pure heart? Is it possible to have a pure heart? There are many questions that can be asked concerning a pure heart, but the Word sums it up beautifully. In the Bible, it says, *"The fining pot is for silver, and the furnace for gold; but the LORD tries the hearts"* (Proverbs 17:3 KJV).

HE'S not talking about your physical heart; HE'S talking about the true you, your spirit. When our spirit was cut off from our connection to our Creator from the fall of man, our soul (which is our mind) and our will became our dominant mode of operation.

We know that when gold and silver go through the refining process, they come out pure. The process may take time. It may be hard to clean, and it won't end until it's perfect. That is liken to what GOD is doing with our hearts. Every day, we are in the finery pot, working and working to get just a little bit purer than the day before, by studying GOD'S Word, by speaking faith-filled words, and having pure thoughts that line up with the Word of GOD, so that we can apply what we learn to our everyday lives. Some days are easier than others, but they still count toward purifying our hearts.

Can you remember a time in your life when you experienced a lot of pain or fear because you didn't know what to do next? This is where you're either in the fining pot or you're in the furnace. Either one will get you closer and closer to being what GOD has ordained for your life. It's not a destination; it's a journey. We will never arrive but will always get better and better.

Recently, I had a situation play out with someone that I thought was a friend. I was hurt deeply by something she did to me. Instead of going to her and telling her how I felt about the situation, I decided to do something that I knew she wouldn't like as well. After I did this, I was so conflicted, I couldn't get it off my mind. I knew what she did to me was wrong, but I knew that what I did was wrong too. I should have taken the high ground, but instead, I stooped down to her level and did what I knew was wrong. Finally, when I saw her again, I went up to her and asked forgiveness for what I had done. She accepted my apology but didn't admit her wrongdoing in the matter. It was okay, because I learned from this; I grew from this experience, and I was able to pray for her, that one day she would also learn and grow from this experience. I can say that this was like being in the refining pot and some cleaning had taken place. I feel so much better, and I know I will remember this if it ever crosses my path again.

When I pray now, I ask GOD for a pure heart. I ask HIM to show me where I've fallen short, so that I can work on fixing that area of my life. It has helped me see the beam in my own eye, way before trying to get the speck out of someone else's. The Bible says, *"Keep thy heart with all diligence; for out of it are the issues of life"* (Proverbs 4:23 KJV).

You can have a pure heart; you just must be intentional and committed to working on yourself and apply the Word in all your life situations.

Chapter 8

Eyes Haven't Seen; Ears Haven't Heard

"But as it is written, eye hath not seen nor ear heard, neither hath entered into the heart of woman, the things which GOD hath prepared for them that love HIM."
(1 Corinthians 2:9)

Your Dreams Speak

Did you know that our FATHER loves to talk to us? That's what HE did with Adam every day in the garden of Eden, and HE'S still doing this today with those who allow HIM, by being still long enough to hear him. Sometimes, we get so busy in our day-to-day life activities that we can only hear our kids screaming in the background when we're on the phone with the repairman, because water is shooting out everywhere! We just don't hear HIM because we don't know what HIS voice sounds like.

There are many examples in the Bible where GOD spoke to HIS servants in their dreams or night visions. HE spoke to Abraham through a night vision, showing him the stars and what it would mean for his future. HE spoke to Moses, Joshua, Isaac, and Jacob.

When HE spoke to Joseph in his dream, and he shared it with his brothers, they didn't believe what he said; they even got a little offended about what he said, because it implied that they would bow down to him. Since they didn't have a total understanding of the dream, they didn't receive it well.

Everyone dreams at night. It is a scientific fact that at certain times during our sleep, we dream. Sometimes, we remember all our dreams; sometimes, we don't remember any of our dreams. But we still dream. Your dreams have meaning, and your dreams have value. I believe that because we are made in HIS image, and HIS Word says so, HE is speaking to you and me in our dreams and night visions.

Your dreams are powerful. They reveal so much of your life journey that you can explore and receive much love and reward from, but only if you believe. Belief is the key. If you believe GOD is speaking to you in your dreams, then you will receive blessings from your dreams. If you don't believe HE is, then you will miss out on the blessings from your dreams.

I have a "dream program" that I use to help my clients hear what the LORD is saying to them when they dream at night. I show them how the answers to the challenges they are having in their day hours, are revealed in their night hours in their dreams. It's amazing how accurate your dreams are to help you solve your life situations and live a more fulfilled life. I offer all my clients a FREE dream session to start the ball rolling to understand where they are and where they want to be. You can have this free resource too. Just contact me at www.theinspiredwomanbook.com.

To show you how GOD speaks in your dreams, here is an example of a dream that I had. One day my daughter and I got into a heated conversation about her driving my 2-day-old new car. She was only 16 years old and had totaled my old car, which is why I had to get a new car. We went back and forth about why I would not let her drive my new car. She felt entitled and that I was being selfish. I said, "No, that's not why." When I was growing up, my father always said, "Never let anyone drive your car if they do not have the finances to fix or replace your car if something happens when they are driving your car." That always stuck with me.

That night I had a dream. In the dream, I was walking down the street on the sidewalk, and a car full of teenagers pulled up and rolled their window down and asked me if I knew how to drive a stick-shift. I told them, "Yes." As I was trying to explain to them how to synchronize the clutch and the gas so that it would be a smooth transition, they got impatient, waved their hand at me, and said, "Forget it!"

Then they took off. I could hear the clutch burning out. After taking a few more steps down the street, I heard and saw them hit a fire hydrant. Then I heard the LORD speak and say, "She needs more experience before you let her drive." I got my answer. I did the right thing by not letting her drive my car.

Your dreams are speaking to you. They have the wisdom and answers you are looking for. This is one of the best kept secrets that no one is talking about. When you learn how to unveil the mystery of your dreams, you will be unstoppable. Sometimes, I can't wait to go to sleep because I know I am going to receive some good nuggets to help me with my life challenges today.

I love working with my clients to help them understand their dreams and apply them to their lives so that they can walk in victory in those areas. It's so exciting to see the light bulb come on when you know that the dream you had last night has just shown you exactly what to do. If you would like to learn more about dream interpretation, just contact me at www.theinspiredwomanbook.com, and I will send you a free blueprint that will help you get started.

It's Not Just a Sign on the Road

Have you ever had something going on in your life and it was so big of a challenge that you just couldn't see how you were going to make it through? You prayed day and night, looking for your answers, but nothing seemed to make sense to you so that you could solve your problem. Finally, when you just couldn't take it anymore, or time was running out, you were so nervous that you couldn't sit still. Here's a made-up story to help you see how signs can happen anywhere and anytime.

You're driving and you come to a red light. You stop, glance over, and you see a truck stopped in front of you. It has a sign on the back that reads, "Call him." You just had that thought of calling your Uncle Bob. He had told you years ago that if you ever needed him, he would be there for you, but you didn't want to call him because he was going through a lot of health problems too. So, you erased that thought from your mind. Now, you're at your wits end and don't know what to do, and you see the truck in front of you saying, "Call him!" You find it hard to believe! You rub your eyes because you think, maybe, you're seeing things that aren't there. When you open your eyes, it's still there. You now stare at the sign as the light turns green, saying to yourself, "That sign just gave me my answer!" It wasn't just a sign. It was the HOLY SPIRIT using something natural to get you to see something SPIRIT wants you to know or do, so that you can accomplish what you need to get done.

GOD is answering your prayers because of your belief and faith. Almost every day, there are signs that have your answers in them. As a born-again believer, you not only have natural eyes and ears; you also have spiritual eyes and ears. When you learn and practice using your spiritual eyes and ears, you will receive so much more than you asked for.

Girl, You're Blessed Coming in and Out

You are so blessed! Your FATHER set up blessings for you even before HE formed you in your mother's womb. In Deuteronomy, Chapter twenty-eight, GOD poured out all the blessings that shall overtake you, when you are diligent to observe and do all HIS commandments that HE commands us to do.

Some teach that the New Testament replaces the Old Testament, but that is not so. YESHUA is the fulfillment of the Old Testament. Therefore, without the Old Testament, there would be no New Testament. The more we learn and understand the Old Testament, the more we will receive from the New Testament. So, all the blessings that GOD said in Deuteronomy twenty-eight still stands for us who diligently harken unto the voice of our LORD and SAVIOR. The Bible says, *"All these blessings shall come upon them and overtake them if thou shalt hearken unto the vice of the LORD thy GOD"* (Deuteronomy 28:2 KJV).

This means that we have ears to hear in the Spirit. Our spiritual ears can hear our LORD, our GOD. Now after we hear, we must be diligent. Being diligent means that we must continually hear and do what the LORD tells us. These are the requirements for the blessings to flow and overtake us. If the requirements aren't met, then you will not experience the flow of "overtake" in your life. But don't you know? HE has already blessed you so much up until now in your life. HE'S still blessing you. Every day, you are awakened with your right mind, a mind to serve HIM and give HIM glory! Praise GOD! He never stops blessing you every day, more and more! HE'S such an awesome GOD. HE loves you so much! All HE wants is for you to choose to serve HIM and then let HIM pour out HIS love on you every day. Deuteronomy is just a small portion of what HE does or will do for you. Do you love HIM? Will you let HIM love you?

I love HIM with all I could ever ask or think! When I think about the many things HE has done for me, I can't hold back the tears. There were many times I should have been dead, in a mental hospital, raped, molested, jailed, abused, shot, homeless, penniless, jobless, and more. I cannot count how many times HE saved me, even before I knew HIM as my LORD and SAVIOR.

I AM grateful for all the trials and tribulations I endured that caused me to one day cry out to HIM to take my life, and instead of taking my life, HE SAVED ME! What false god would have done all this for me? What false god would have died on the cross just for me? I live because HE lives! HE is my everything and more. Every day when I say that I love HIM, HE always says back to me, *"Eyes haven't seen, ear haven't heard, all the wonderful things I have prepared for you."* We do this together every day. Why? Because we have a relationship; we spend time with each other. HE loves it when I put HIM before everything else in this world and just love on HIM and let HIM love on me.

I walk in faith every day because I know that's what HE wants me to do, so that I won't stop the blessings HE'S sending me for that day! I'm blessed everywhere I go; HE told me that my hands are blessed, and everything I touch will be blessed. That's why if we ever get a chance to meet, I hope you will let me touch you, with a hug or a handshake, because I know I'm doing what HE asked me to do: bless HIS people.

My sisters, hear me when I say, GOD loves you so much! It's time for you to go deeper in your understanding. HE knew Eve was going to do what she did in the garden of Eden; HE knew satan would hate women all around the world, and do terrible things to babies, young girls, and women. HE knew that he would want to destroy every baby girl, young girl, and woman.

For that reason, GOD had a plan. This plan is deep. Many women don't know or understand GOD'S plan for us. The plan is for women that know their identity, to submit their will to HIM, without question, stay in HIS presence all day, every day, sing praises to HIM, and love on HIM. Saturate your heart and mind with HIS Word in prayer. When you do these things, you will experience faith at a whole new level. The joy that will rise in you will be earth-shattering; it will move mountains.

You may be saying to yourself right now that you are already doing these things, or this isn't something new. If you are saying this right now, then that is your proof that you will not experience this until you change your attitude and humble yourself in the presence of the ALMIGHTY GOD. I never said it was new; I said, "GOD has a plan." See, this is the reason women do not experience the deeper revelation of why women are where we are. But GOD is ready to change all of that.

In the Book of Joel, HE said, *"And it shall come to pass afterward that I will pour out my SPIRIT upon all flesh; and your sons and your daughters shall prophesy, your old men shall dream dreams, your young men shall see visions. And, upon the servants and upon the handmaids in those days will I pour out my SPIRIT"* (Joel 2:28-29 KJV). We are now in the "those days" spoken by Joel in this verse. Look around you—look at the women, look at the young women, look at the babies—do you not see it? The breakthrough always comes right when things are at the worst they've ever been. It's time; it's time to step up and be the called women, to accept GOD'S plan for us, so that we can walk in victory and lead our families to the Kingdom.

I know this is my call. I know I have been chosen. Do you? When we step into our rightful position, GOD is going to release an anointing upon all of us, that will shatter the nations. I feel the anointing as I'm writing these words. As a prophet, I will not say or write anything that the HOLY SPIRIT doesn't tell me to write or say. This is one of those times. When I woke up this morning to write this chapter, I did not know HE was going to take me in this direction. I thank you LORD for what you're doing with my hands right now! Ladies, I work with women. I lead women who know that they are chosen for a greater work. If that's you, then it is not by accident that you are reading my book. You are chosen too. But you probably already knew that. Well, I'm confirming it for you! I've prayed for you, I know you, I care for you, and I love you. You are special to GOD. HE wants to bring you to a special place in HIM; a place you have never seen before.

Women have been abused for so long that it's hard to trust and know when something is good for us. The LORD wants you to know that HE'S changing all of that, HE wants you to know that HE has you in HIS arms, and HE is waiting for you to receive HIS love without doubt and fear. Your life is about to change. You are stepping into your now!

Now faith is here! Just receive it! Ahh, I can't wait until my retreat, where I can gather all of you and teach you how to experience GOD at a whole new level. It's going to be life-changing. Remember to reach out to me so that I can send you some resources that will bless you and your family, at www.theinspiredwomanbook.com.

You're Healed and Highly Favored

I remember, some years ago, when I was confused about who I was in CHRIST. I had just given my life to CHRIST, and I was excited and on fire for the LORD. Because I was a new babe in CHRIST, I didn't know about the gifts of the SPIRIT. I didn't know that GOD had already chosen me to operate in certain gifts and talents. So, when I would go to church, I would start noticing certain things happening to me. I attended a deliverance ministry church, under the late Bishop Ralph E. Green, in Coral Hills, Maryland. That is where I got saved and delivered from so many things. Being under his ministry, I saw all the gifts of the SPIRIT operating in the services. There were two things that happened to me every time I went to church. One was when certain people came down to the altar for healing prayer. Wherever they had pain in their body, I would feel it in my body. Sometimes, it would have me hunched over as they were. After Bishop Green lay hands on them and prayed for them, I could feel when they received their healing. My husband noticed this happening to me too. He would look at me strangely, as if he was asking me, "Are you feeling that?" He and I both knew it was happening.

The second gift I noticed when I went to church, was the interpretation of tongues. This didn't happen every time, but enough to know I should pay attention to it. Thirty years ago, speaking in tongues wasn't as well-known as it is today. There has been so much debate around "the gift of tongues" and the indwelling or being filled with the HOLY SPIRIT, as the SPIRIT gives the utterance. Some think these are the same; some believe they are different. I believe the latter.

In the Book of Acts, *"Paul, passing through the upper coasts came to Ephesus, found some believers and he asked them, 'Have you received the HOLY SPIRIT since you believed?' And they said, 'We have not heard whether there be any HOLY SPIRIT'"* (ACTS 19:1-2 KJV). That tells me that after you believe, the next step is to be filled with the HOLY SPIRIT. Peter, also in the Book of Acts, spoke the plan of salvation to the people. He said, in Acts Chapter 2 verse 38, *"... repent, and be baptized every one of you in the name of YESHUA the CHRIST for the remission of sins, and ye shall receive the gift of the HOLY SPIRIT"* (KJV).

It's not until you receive this gift of the HOLY SPIRIT, that you will truly understand that you need this to live and have relationship with GOD ALMIGHTY. In all thy getting, get understanding.

Hear the Sound of GOD

There is a sound that is of GOD. Many do not know it, but it is there. It can only be heard with your spiritual ears. It can only be heard if you are saved and filled with HIS SPIRIT. This sound is important, because when HE calls you, you must obey. How can you obey if you don't hear him? The sound is unique to you. It's your sound that GOD has placed in you. When you hear it and truly listen to it, it will take you somewhere else. The sound is like a vibration, and vibrations are always moving on wave lengths. When you sit still long enough and tune everything else out of your thoughts, you can start to think about YESHUA, put your mind on HIM, and you will hear the sound. It's a still, small sound that will arise in your spirit. As you practice listening, it will become stronger and clearer for you. It's important for you to know this sound because this sound will save your life one day.

Have you ever had an experience where you were supposed to go somewhere or do something on a given day, but at the last minute, you changed your mind for whatever reason? Something put that thought into your mind, to not go down that street or to not go to work that day. You thought it was just you thinking out loud, but if you go back and remember the whole incident, you might remember that you heard a sound or felt a feeling right before you changed your mind to do or not to do the thing.

Many people call this "your gut or your intuition," but I call it hearing the sound of GOD, or hearing the HOLY SPIRIT. Trust GOD, trust HIS SPIRIT; trust GOD, trust HIS sound. Trust the HOLY SPIRIT to lead and guide you into all truth.

I remember when the policeman told me to give him the drugs that I had in my pocket. When I look back on it now, I did hear a sound, then a small voice that told me to give it to him. It was scary because I had never been in that situation before, but I surrendered to the unknown, and it saved my life. Now, I'm always listening to see if that sound is there before I embark on something I've never done before.

You Shall Live and Not Die

In the United States, depression is one of the most diagnosed conditions, especially among young people and people in their mid-thirties. I want you to repeat after me: "I SHALL LIVE AND NOT DIE!" The Bible says, *"Death and life are in the power of the tongue, and they that love it, shall eat the fruit thereof"* (Proverbs 18:21 KJV).

A few years ago, I traveled to Michigan to attend our family reunion. One evening, while I was in town, my cousin invited us over for a cookout at his house. I met his new wife and stepdaughter. She was in her 2nd or 3rd year of college, and she was real sweet too. On the outside, she looked like a normal twenty-year-old: smiling, happy, and well taken care of. A few days after we got back home to Maryland, I received a call stating that the young lady had committed suicide. Her mother walked into her bedroom and saw her child hanging from the ceiling. I was in shock! I couldn't believe this! This young lady was an A student, worked hard, and was obedient to her parents. There were no signs that she was sad or depressed, until they found the note. In the note, the young lady said that she was under so much pressure to succeed that she didn't believe she could live up to her family's expectations of her.

Our young people have so many things to deal with now that weren't around when we were children. They have incurable sexual diseases, and intense peer pressure due to the rise of social media. There are manmade drugs being spread around, and even pharmaceutical drugs have easy accessibility. All these things combined have created an atmosphere where they feel like they don't have a way out.

We know that's a lie; we know the enemy wants to destroy them and their futures. He wants them to feel hopeless and defeated so that he can control them and get them to kill themselves or kill others. Now is the time that we must speak life over ourselves and over our children as soon as they are born. Tell them every day, "I love you; YESHUA loves you." Plant the seeds of love and life every day.

You are fearfully and wonderfully made by the ALMIGHTY GOD. HE created you to live, and live life abundantly. HE has given you joy—unspeakable joy. Walk in joy and peace every day. This is your birth right, your inheritance. Let nothing take this from you. You are amazing! You are blessed and highly favored! All good things come from above from our FATHER, who does exceedingly above all that we can ask or think. HE loves you with an everlasting love. HE will never leave you, nor forsake you. Walk in HIS love and peace always.

Chapter 9

Inspiration Comes From Within

"All Scripture is given by inspiration of GOD, and is profitable for doctrine, for reproof, for correction, for instruction in righteousness."
(2 Timothy 3:16)

I AM Inspired to Be More Like CHRIST

There is a difference between motivation and inspiration. Sometimes, people believe they are the same, but they're not. People listen to motivational speakers in the hope that it will inspire them to do something they long for or dream about doing. I say, no one can motivate you; you must motivate yourself.

Motivation comes from outside influences, but inspiration comes from within. That is why I named this book, *The Inspired Woman.* My desire is that after you read these words, you will be internally inspired to go and live your dreams, making all of them come true. It's not easy to stay motivated about a dream or a goal you are working on. Motivation comes and goes. But when you are inspired about something, you will stay the course, even after the motivation has died down. You will wake up every morning thinking about your goals and your dreams.

Somehow, inspiration compels you to keep going, no matter what it looks like. What is this inner inspiration that you feel? It's the HOLY SPIRIT; it's CHRIST. CHRIST is always pushing you to become more like HIM, so that you will fulfill your destiny HE created you for. You are an "Inspired Woman!" You are becoming more and more CHRIST-like. Your true self is SPIRIT; GOD is SPIRIT, and the two became one when you gave your life to CHRIST. Now, your desires are active, and you can feel them. These desires are driving you, inspiring you to do all the things you hope and dream of doing.

You Have Abundant Life

Do you know you have an abundant life right now? You have had it from the very first breath you took. Your FATHER in Heaven said in HIS Word, *"... I AM come that they might have life, and that they might have it more abundantly"* (John 10:10 KJV).

You must let this be your mindset. Mindset is your way of thinking; it is your opinion about things. But the Bible tells us to put on the mind of CHRIST, to let this mind of CHRIST be in you. Every day, say out loud to yourself, "I have the mind of CHRIST." This is abundance. Abundance is eternal. There is no beginning or end. When you were born again in CHRIST, you received eternal life; you received abundant life.

Now that you have abundance, everything changes. You no longer think like the world thinks, because you have the mind of CHRIST. You no longer act like the world; meaning, you stop doing things that are sinful and contrary to GOD'S Word. The mind of CHRIST changes you. You can feel the changes. You have confidence because you know without doubt that you have changed. You feel the abundance operating in your life. You see it everywhere you go; it's alive and it's freeing. Your life has new meaning. You know your purpose and you feel the joy down in your heart; it makes you very happy. You feel free—free to be your true self and to let others be the same.

You are learning more and more about yourself and how to live better, be better, and to give and share with the love of CHRIST that's overflowing in your heart. This abundant life is spilling over in every area of your life and people are noticing a difference in you. You're more positive, happy, loving, giving, and they feel good around you.

The more you believe and have faith that you have an abundant life, the more truth will be revealed to confirm this. You are living an abundant life every day because you know who you are, you believe GOD, and you choose to walk in abundance.

Joy, Unspeakable Joy

"Lift up your heads, O ye gates; and be ye lifted up, ye everlasting doors; and the KING of glory shall come in. Who is this KING of glory? The LORD strong and mighty..."
(Psalm 24:7-8 KJV)

This joy I have, the world didn't give it to me, and the world cannot take it from me. There are nine fruits of the SPIRIT, and one of them is joy—unspeakable joy. We say, "The joy of the LORD is my strength." What does that really mean? It means, when everything around you is falling apart in all areas of your life, you can't explain why, but your heart is filled with joy.

Imagine waking up in the morning with thanksgiving in your heart and a big smile on your face. You get to work, and the boss calls you into his office and tells you that they are downsizing and he's terminating your position. You still have a smile on your face. He looks at you puzzled, because he just fired you, but you are still smiling. The world cannot comprehend this joy that you have, because they didn't give it to you, and they cannot take it from you. What the boss doesn't know is that the joy of the LORD is your strength and that you have joy, unspeakable joy. You walk out of his office feeling better than you did when you walked into his office. You're smiling while cleaning out your desk and walking out the front door because you know GOD has a plan—a plan to prosper you and do you good all the days of your life.

Your hope and faith are in CHRIST. You allow joy to flow and manifest daily in your life. You are strong and receive all the strength joy provides for you, so that everything GOD has for you can be established in your life right now.

I AM Inspired to Be, Do, and Have

A few years ago, my sister lived in the same city as I did. Every week, she would ask me to take a walk with her, and every week, I turned her down. I always came up with one excuse or another just to say no to the walk. She didn't know the real reason I was saying no to her. I kept the real reason from her.

I was living a sedentary lifestyle: sitting at my desk all day, every day, and was experiencing pain in my left foot and my back. One day I went to church and the woman of GOD prayed for my foot. That was the last day I had pain in my foot. YESHUA healed me completely. By that time, my sister had moved 30-plus miles away from my city and she didn't ask me to go walking with her anymore.

Then one glorious day, as I was looking out of my window, I had a thought (I thought it was me, but it really was the HOLY SPIRIT who gave me this thought). "I'm going for a walk." I got up, got dressed, put on the right shoes for walking, and set out to walk. Well, very quickly, I started to think I had made a mistake, and this was a bad idea. My lower back started hurting worse than it ever had before. I was only 3 or 5 minutes into my walk. I said to myself, "Girl, how are you going to do this when you can't even walk 5 minutes without pain?"

Do you know what inspired me to keep going? My family. I started thinking, if there was some kind of emergency and we needed to run to escape the danger, I wouldn't be able to do it. I would have to beg them to leave without me or all of us wouldn't make it. This thought inspired me that it was time to change; it was time for me to BE the woman, wife, and mother I needed to be so that we all could live a better life.

So, I put on my big girl shoes, struggled through the pain of day one, and I walked for ten minutes! I was so proud of myself. I did it! I made it through one day. The next day, I was committed to doing even better than the day before. One day turned into one week. One week turned into 30 days straight. I started walking now for 30 minutes a day. Then I had another thought, "Could I walk every day for one year straight?" Well, guess what? As of writing this book to date, I have walked over 760 days, for 1 to 2+ miles per day! If you would have asked me 2 years ago if I would walk every day for the rest of my life, I would have told you, "No way!" But now I can see a vision of myself walking every day for the rest of my life, or until these legs can't carry me any further.

I am so inspired to walk. It started out that I was doing it for me, but now it has taken on so much more meaning. When I learned that my brother had one of his legs amputated, I knew then that I wanted to walk for those who couldn't walk. Now, not only do I walk for them, but now I walk for spiritual reasons. GOD is using my legs to intercede on behalf of HIS people. I walk for souls to be healed, delivered, and set free. I walk for unborn babies, and children that have been abused and molested. I walk for young girls who are trafficked and lost. I walk for the Body of CHRIST to come into the full knowledge of the Kingdom of GOD. There is so much we can do, be, and have when we let the HOLY SPIRIT use us for HIS glory. Be inspired; let your light shine so that others can see the light, and be drawn to the CHRIST in you! You are everything you were inspired to be, do, and have! I bless you, and I thank you for inspiring me to write these words.

I AM Strong

You are so much stronger than you think you are. The Bible says, *"... the joy of the LORD is your strength"* (Nehemiah 8:10 KJV). Walk in your strength. This strength you have did not come from you; it came from GOD. HE told Joshua, *"Be strong and of a good courage"* (Joshua 1:6 KJV). HE gave Samson supernatural physical strength. There are so many instances where people have done things they didn't know they could do.

Every year, I sell gift baskets for Mother's Day. One year, I was out selling my baskets and a young mom and her two- or three-year-old daughter approached my table to see the gifts. My table was in a parking lot outside, not far from the street. As they came up to my table, I was closer to the street than they were. She was holding her daughter's hand when she approached my table, but when she saw a gift basket that she liked, she let go of her daughter's hand to pick it up. Immediately, the little girl took off running. She ran into the street. Without a second thought, I took off running to grab the little girl. I caught her just as we both were in the middle of the intersection of the street. When I grabbed her and looked up, a truck driver had jammed on their brakes and stopped just in time to not hit us. I was in shock that I had caught her and we did not get hit. I never knew I could run that fast! I know it was strength that GOD had given me so that I could save this little girl from being hit by the truck. I thank GOD every day for life, health, and strength!

You are strong, you are powerful, and you have everything you need to live a wonderful life. Don't be afraid to live. Don't be afraid to live your dreams! Go, go, go—do that thing you've always wanted to do. You can do it! I know you can, because I did it! GOD is no respecter of any one person. What HE does for one, HE can do for you! I believe in you, because I believe GOD. You believe GOD, and you know you can do all things in CHRIST who strengthens you!

Renew and Transform Your Mind

Your faith runs deep inside you. It's a reflection of who you really are. The beauty of faith is that GOD has already given you a measure of faith, but you must be in alignment with it to see it bring forth abundance of everything in your life. Faith can renew and transform you from the inside out.

Let's look at Sarah. She had wanted a child for many, many years. When she was a young girl, she probably used to daydream about her life and when she would have her first child, and then her second, and so on. Her belief levels were high; she had no reason to doubt that she would have children. Then, as the years passed by, after being married for many years, her faith and belief started to wear down.

She started having more and more doubt about whether she would ever have children. Her thoughts might have constantly been, "When will I have a child? Why haven't I conceived yet? What's wrong with me?"

All these thoughts turned her faith back the opposite way of receiving blessings. Her mind was renewed into believing the opposite of what she really wanted. It even caused her to make decisions that brought on even bigger problems in her life. She lived for years with this new mindset, that she would never have children because she was too old. But GOD!

In this story, we know the angels came to visit Sarah's husband, Abraham, and after their meeting, the angel asked Abraham, "Where is your wife Sarah?" The angel then said, "She shall bear a son by this time next year." Sarah heard this and laughed! The angel heard her laugh, and asked Sarah, "Why did you laugh?" She then tried to deny it but could not. Because of her mindset, she couldn't release her faith to believe what the angel had said to them. She was stuck in her current situation; meaning, only looking in the natural world, and she couldn't receive what was being revealed in the spiritual realm.

We know that the promises of GOD are "yes and amen." Even if it's not humanly possible in the natural world for something to happen, it's not impossible in the spiritual realm. GOD will always do what HE promises to do. You can take that to the bank and cash it! Let this mind be in you, which also is in CHRIST. Renew your mind with the Word of GOD. HIS Word will transform you and set you free from all the lies of this world. When you think supernaturally, you can receive supernaturally.

Chapter 10

I Have Kept the Faith

10

***"But the path of the just is as the shining light, that shineth more and more unto the perfect day."* (Proverbs 4:18 KJV)**

Keep Walking by Faith and Not by Sight

We have come this far by faith! You have kept the faith! You are strong; you are full of joy. No more fear, no more doubt. You know exactly what to do and what not to do. Your faith is strong; you are growing stronger and stronger in your faith. You believe beyond a shadow of a doubt that all things work for the good of them that are called of HIM. No one can shake you or move you out of your belief and faith in GOD'S will for your life. You know that no matter what comes your way, you will be strong enough, have faith enough, and belief enough to overcome it. You are walking strong in faith. You know you're on the path that HE created just for you. You see only the truth; the voice of a stranger, you will not follow. You know HIS voice; you see with your spiritual eyes, not your natural eyes. Your sight is keen, developed to discern good and evil, so that you can keep steady on the course that leads to an abundant life. Every day you wake up knowing that this day will bring more love, peace, joy, and faith into your life. You can see all the blessings raining down on you. It feels so wonderful, you can't contain it. It spreads all around you and you share it with others. Every day is a new day of love and power to see the fruit of your labor manifest in every area of your life. You hear GOD. You feel love, joy, and peace. Everything is changing in your life. You no longer have headaches and panic attacks. Your body is healing itself physically, mentally, and spiritually. Your family is puzzled; they are scratching their heads and trying to figure out why you are so different and why you are so happy. You can't stop singing and smiling, because you walk by faith and not by sight!

Every Morning, You Have New Mercy

GOD loves us so much that HE always makes a way of escape for us. No matter what we put ourselves into, HE always, always gives us new mercy to rise and be victorious in it. Every day, when you rise and praise HIM and have gratitude for all the things HE'S done in your life, you receive HIS grace and mercy to go on; to not stop, to win, and to receive all the blessings. As you seek HIM early when you awaken, and ask for forgiveness of all sin you may have committed knowingly or unknowingly, HE'S faithful and just to forgive all your sins. Now you're ready to receive;

your faith is strong, your belief is strong, and your confidence is strong. You are ready for your marching orders for the day.

I remember a time in my life when I had unforgiveness in my heart toward my husband. There were things I wanted him to do, and he just wouldn't do them. I got mad and tried to manipulate situations to try and get him to do what I wanted. This was wrong; I knew it was wrong, but I wanted what I wanted. When things got even worse because of what I did, I finally realized the magnitude of what I was doing, and I fell to my knees and cried out to the LORD to forgive me for the sins I had committed and for the unforgiveness I had in my heart toward my husband.

Because I was sincere in wanting forgiveness from GOD and my husband, I immediately felt freedom from the weight of this sin. I repented of everything I knew I had done and what I didn't remember that I had done. I knew GOD'S mercy had set me free! I now can walk in new mercy and start over with a clean slate, turn around, and go the right way to mend my heart and relationship with the LORD and my husband.

Mercy is a wonderful thing! It changes our hearts; it moves obstacles out of our way so that we can walk boldly in GOD'S love and grace. GOD'S mercy and grace are there for you. Receive it now!

Be Strong and Courageous

The Bible tells us *"to be strong and courageous"* (Joshua 1:6-7 KJV). GOD didn't tell us this just because it sounds good. No, HE told Joshua this because HE meant it! HE even repeated it to him several times so that he could build his faith and get him ready for the battles ahead. Joshua was about to embark on a journey that would take him and all of GOD'S people into places they could never imagine they would go to; places where everything is different. They needed to get ready. They needed to be prepared for the journey ahead; so, Joshua, being the leader, had to get his mindset developed and ready for what was ahead. GOD took the time and prepared him so that he would be able to lead in victory. Being strong and courageous is not an option; it's a command from GOD. GOD was only letting Joshua see all the strength he had already placed in him. When Joshua started seeing it in his spiritual eyes, his belief and faith started growing. He could feel something different stirring up inside of him. He saw boldness in himself. His shoulders were back and he stood up tall and straight; his head was raised high, and nothing could stop him now. He was ready, he was prepared, and he was strong!

This is you! GOD has already told you what to do next. HE has given you the answer, in your dream or when you saw the sign on the truck, or when HE spoke through a child, or when HE spoke directly to you. Go do the thing

HE told you to do! You already know what it is, but because it's something you've never done before, you shy away from getting started. It's now time; it's your time to step out in faith and do it scared, do it lonely, and do it when you don't know what to do—just do something.

Be strong and be of good courage, and you will see GOD'S strength working on your behalf. You always have more than you think you have. Use that and let it start you moving toward your goals and dreams.

HE'S Always with You

Have you ever experienced a time in your life when you were going through a very hard trial and you felt a presence all around you? A good presence—peaceful, relaxed, and with no stress? A feeling of knowing everything was going to work out fine?

When I was consumed by my addiction to drugs, I would do almost anything to get drugs for that day. It was around 1 a.m. in the morning and I had no more drugs to get high on. A friend of mine said, "Hey, let's ride into DC and score some more, but you go with these guys, and I will stay here and watch the kids." So, I jumped in the car with 3 people I had just met. I didn't even know their names. It was a cold January night, probably one of the coldest nights I can ever remember there in the DC area. It felt like I was back in Michigan! As the driver got to the neighborhood where he would make the purchase, he slowed down, stopped, and then asked a man on the roadside where he could get some PCP or cocaine. The man said, "I got you; you can get it here. How much do you want?" I was in the back seat so I couldn't hear or see everything that was going on, but what I did see was unbelievable.

The next thing I heard was that the driver switched the original bag and gave the dealer a fake bag of marijuana and cocaine, saying he didn't want it. The dealer saw him switch the bags and threatened to kill everyone in the car for trying to deceive him and steal his merchandise. Suddenly, four more men approached the car with bats in their hands and started to smash in the windows of the car. They were screaming, "I'm going to kill you; I'm going to drag you out of this car and kill all of you!"

I couldn't believe what was happening right before my eyes! I was going to be killed all because I got in a car with people I had never seen before, who were trying to steal from drug dealers. I was so afraid! I was helpless. They were making progress in getting the windows busted out and soon started pulling the driver out of the car.

Right then, a miracle happened! The lady in front of me recognized the man who was beating the window out on her side of the car; it was her cousin. She started pleading with him, saying, "Hey, you're my cousin; let us out, let us out." He stopped hitting the window and recognized her too, and said, "Yeah, that's my cousin. Let her out—those in the back seat too!"

This was the hand of GOD covering me, even when I do things that are crazy! HE was with me, and I did not know it. HE protected me from the hand of evil on that cold January night.

Sister, please know that GOD is always with you! HE will never leave you, nor forsake you! You can trust HIM no matter where you are or what you're doing. Thank you, LORD!

Always Give Love and Be Faithful

Love is the most powerful gift GOD gave us. It's also one of the most misunderstood emotions. The Bible says, *"... faith, hope, and love. But the greatest of these is love."* GOD is love, and HE created us in love; HE wanted us to know love, give love, and love one another. Love covers a multitude of sins. YESHUA died for our sins, yet so many don't believe and accept HIM as their LORD and SAVIOR. If they only knew what real love is; if they only knew the reason why they were conceived and born into this world... it was because of love that this world would be a different place.

I remember when I was around nine or ten and waiting for the bus at the bus stop. There was a family of four who bullied everyone on the bus, especially my sister and me. I remember being so scared to get on the bus that I would shake and almost pee my pants. One day as I was waiting at the bus stop, thinking about what was going to happen when I got on the bus, I had a thought that was so clear in my head that I have never forgotten it even to this day. I said to myself, "How come everybody can't just love each other? It's so simple. All we must do is love each other and everything will be fine for everyone." Out of the mouths of babes!

Love was the answer to my bus problem! Love is the answer to all problems! This is the secret to living a faith-filled life that many do not know. When you discover this secret, your life will change. GOD knew the secret because HE is the secret! YESHUA knew the secret because HE is the secret. Now that you know the secret, what are you going to do about it?

You can use it in your marriage, your business, your family... in all areas of your life. When you have a problem, ask yourself first, "How can I solve this in love?" That's what will open the door to wisdom in love to bring about your solutions from this secret tool that most do not understand and use.

I want to connect with you. Reach out to me at www.theinspiredwomanbook.com and let me know how I can best serve you. I love supporting GOD'S women to learn and grow so that they can live a more GOD-filled life of joy and happiness.

You Have Spiritual Access

Your FATHER wants you to know that there is no good thing HE shall withhold from you! HE is proud of you, and HE has only great things to give and show you. HE only wants you to love HIM, show love, and give love as HE has given unto you. Every time you give love, you're letting your FATHER'S love for you shine through. Always keep your faith strong, and it will keep you strong. Remember to be strong and be courageous. Your FATHER will never leave you. HE loves you so much that HE died just for you. HE has given you everything HE has. HE has given you HIS best! Your strength is HIS strength. Do everything with prayer and supplication. Seek first the Kingdom of GOD and HIS righteousness, and all other things will be added. The joy of the LORD will always be your strength. Weeping may endure for a moment, but joy comes every morning.

Your faith Is a gift from GOD! HE wants you to use It for everything in your life. Use your faith every day, from the time you wake up until the time you lie down to sleep.

Open your mouth and shout declarations of your faith! Let the world know you are walking in love and faith today.

Finally, love yourself. Be kind to others. Show and teach others that when you love and give love, you bring heaven down to Earth. Then love will spread around the world and heal and deliver GOD'S people from evil. This is the true meaning of faith. Faith is love. Faith is hope, and faith is a gift GOD gave to us to use and share so that everyone can receive everything they want in life! Amen.

About the Author

Prophet Cyndi is a coach, author, and speaker who is passionate about helping women use their faith and see their dreams come true.

She has worked with women to show them how their dreams hold the answers to their daily challenges, and how they can access that information and bring transformation in every area of their lives. Not only will she capture your heart with her loving smile, but she will also go the extra mile to make sure you receive the wisdom and knowledge you need to succeed.

She is married to her loving husband, Jeffrey. She has two daughters, Stephanie and Joi. She also has a dog named Cassie. She loves to teach crochet and sing praises to YESHUA.

Her company, Kingdom Living Enterprises, specializes in coaching and mentoring women in the Body of CHRIST to develop their mindset to dream, walk in faith, and receive all that GOD has destined for them.

You can reach out to her and learn more about her coaching and mentoring programs on her website at www.theinspiredwomanbook.com. You will find free resources that will bless you too!

For bonuses go to ...

Made in the USA
Columbia, SC
16 September 2024

42412340R00095